QUILTED
WALL HANGINGS

LEISURE ARTS, INC. • Maumelle, Arkansas

Need just that perfect piece to change your room's décor?

We've got the perfect solution - add a wall hanging! Any of these wall hangings will make a dramatic change to any room. And most of these projects are so easy, you'll have it done in no time!

Make it, hang it, and enjoy it!

FaveQuits.com is one of the 50 free cooking and crafting websites in the Prime Publishing community. FaveQuilts features thousands of free quilt patterns, tutorials, tips, articles, giveaways, and more. Their free, daily email newsletter, Piecing It Together, offers quilters inspiration with easy-to-follow patterns, tutorials, and gorgeous photos. FaveQuilts caters to quilters of all skill levels from those just starting out to those who have been quilting for decades. They are proud of the relationships they've built with hundreds of quilt bloggers and companies from around the world and are dedicated to bringing the best content to their loyal and dedicated fans.

The FaveQuilts community is flourishing all over social media from its nearly 100,000 Facebook fans to the 74,000 Pinterest followers to the dozens of tutorials available on their YouTube channel. The active online community allows quilters from all over the world to share what they're working on and receive feedback on their current projects. Quilters also have the opportunity to be published by submitting their original projects and images to the site. With over 30 new articles added to the site each week, there's no shortage of content for the quilting enthusiast to explore.

Raw Edge Appliqué makes for an easy play on a New York Beauty block. This raw edge appliqué method uses washable school glue to place the pieces before stitching. I like the texture the fray of the fabric gets after stitching. This is a great project to use the decorative stitches on the sewing machine.

COMPASS OF BEAUTY

Design by Stephanie Kendron

Finished Wall Hanging Size: 25 1/2" x 25 1/2" (65 cm x 65 cm)

SHOPPING LIST

Yardage is based on 43"/44" (109 cm/112 cm) wide fabric with a usable width of 40" (102 cm). Fat quarters are approximately 22" x 18" (56 cm x 46 cm).

- ☐ 1 3/4 yds (1.6 m) of gray solid fabric for background backing, and binding
- ☐ 1 fat quarter ***each*** of white, purple, and pink fabric
- ☐ 1/4 yd (23 cm) ***each*** of dark teal and turquoise fabric for triangles
- ☐ 1/8 yd (11 cm) of yellow print fabric for triangles
- ☐ scrap of mustard green solid fabric for triangles

You will also need:

- ☐ 30" x 30" (76 cm x 76 cm) piece of batting
- ☐ washable school glue
- ☐ template plastic
- ☐ water-soluble fabric marking pen
- ☐ permanent fine-point pen

CUTTING THE PIECES

*Follow **Rotary Cutting**, page 55, to cut fabric. Cut all strips from the selvage-to-selvage width of the fabric. All measurements include 1/4" seam allowances.*

***Note:** Before starting I recommend starching the fabrics. This will help stabilize the bias of the fabric.*

From gray solid fabric:

- Cut **background** 25 1/2" x 25 1/2".
- Cut **backing** 30" x 30".
- Cut 1 **square for binding** 14" x 14".

From mustard green scrap:

- Cut 1 **strip** 1 1/4" x 22".

CUTTING THE APPLIQUÉS

*Use patterns, page 9, and follow **Making and Using Templates**, page 56, to cut appliqués.*

From white fabric:

- Cut 1 **large circle A.**

From purple fabric:

- Cut 1 **outer ring B.**

From pink fabric:

- Cut 1 **small circle C.**

From dark teal fabric:

- Cut 16 **triangles D.**

From turquoise fabric:

- Cut 16 **triangles D.**

From yellow print fabric:

- Cut 4 **triangles D.**

ASSEMBLING THE WALL HANGING TOP

*Follow **Machine Piecing**, page 56, and **Pressing**, page 58, to make wall hanging top. Use washable school glue to place and hold the pieces for appliquéing. The glue will dry and not show or will wash out easily if needed.*

1. To mark the center of **background**, press in half; press in half again.

2. To mark center of circles, press in half; press in half again.

3. Place a small line of glue on the wrong side of the **large circle** about $^1/_8$" from the edge. With right sides facing up and matching creased center lines, place and hold the large circle on the background fabric. Repeat with **small circle** and **outer ring**.

4. Fold raw edge of **strip** to meet in center on wrong side of fabric; press. Cut two 10" lengths.

5. Place a small line of glue near edges on wrong side of strips. Place strips diagonally across circles.

6. Measure $1^1/_2$" out from the circles and mark with a water-soluble pen all around circle. This will be the guide for the bottom of the inner triangles.

7. Glue the first inner **triangle** on the marked line aligned with the strips in the center. Glue an inner triangle at all strip ends. Glue the other inner triangles using the marked line as a guide.

8. Measure $3^1/_2$" out from the circles and mark all around circle. This will be the guide for the bottom of the middle triangles.

9. Glue the first middle triangle on the marked line between the inner triangles. Glue the remaining middle triangles using the marked line as a guide.

10. Using the strips as a guide, measure $4^3/_4$" out from the circles at each corner and mark. This will be the guide for the bottom of the outer triangles.

11. Glue the outer triangles where marked.

12. Stitch the edges of each circle down $^1/_8$" from fabric edge. Stitch the edges of each center strip down $^1/_8$" from fabric edge. This is a great time to use a decorative stitch.

13. Stitch down each triangle.

COMPLETING THE WALL HANGING

Use $^1/_4$" seam allowances.

1. Follow **Quilting**, page 58, to mark, layer, and quilt as desired.

2. Use the edge of a plate to mark the outer edges of the wall hanging with a water soluble marker to round the edges of the wall hanging.

3. Follow **Making a Hanging Sleeve**, page 60, if a hanging sleeve is desired.

4. Use **square for binding** and follow **Making Continuous Bias Binding**, page 60, to make $1^1/_4$" wide bias binding. Follow **Attaching Binding with Mitered Corners**, page 61, Steps 1, 3, & 6-15, to bind wall hanging.

Wall Hanging Top Diagram

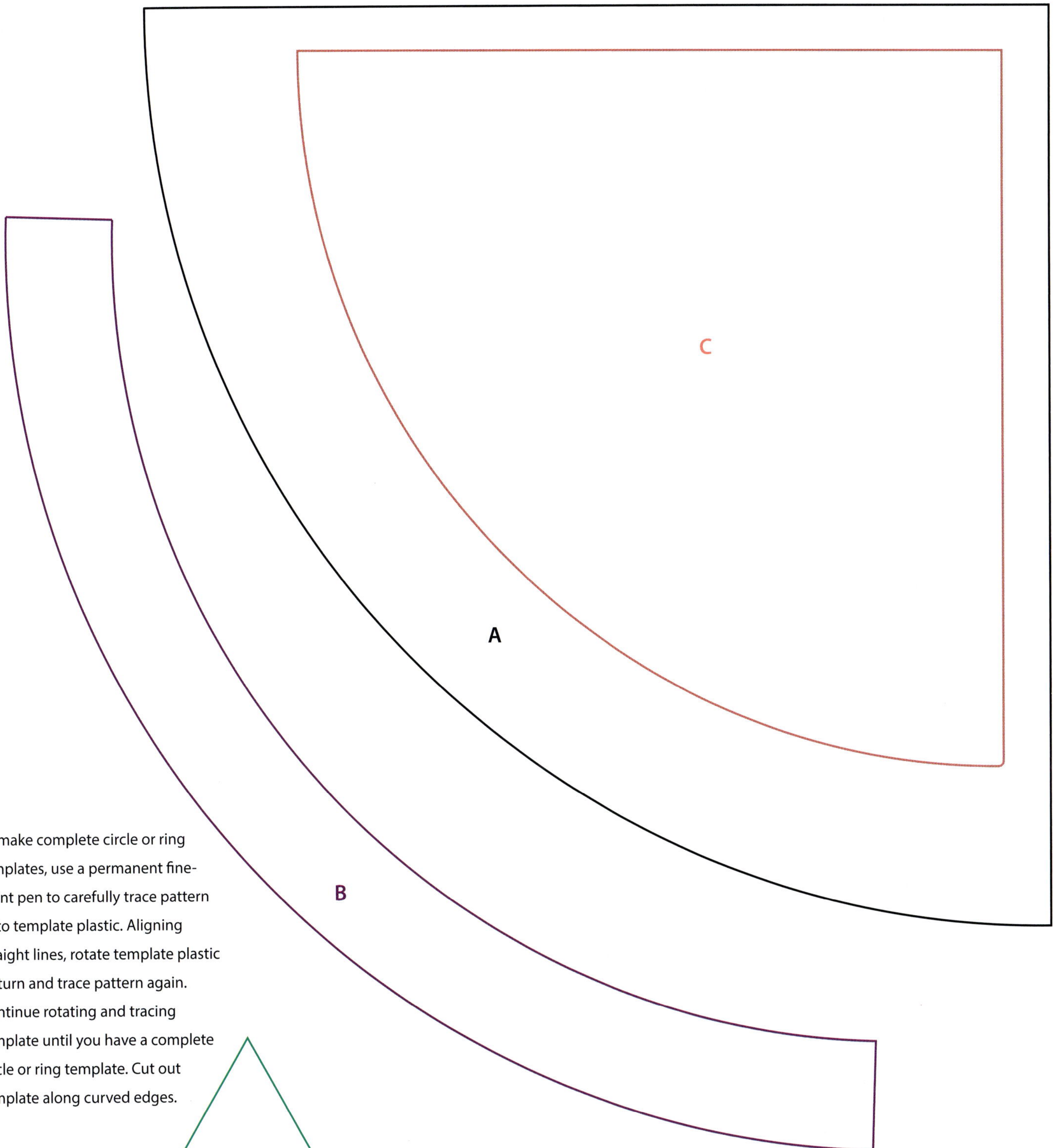

To make complete circle or ring templates, use a permanent fine-point pen to carefully trace pattern onto template plastic. Aligning straight lines, rotate template plastic 1/4 turn and trace pattern again. Continue rotating and tracing template until you have a complete circle or ring template. Cut out template along curved edges.

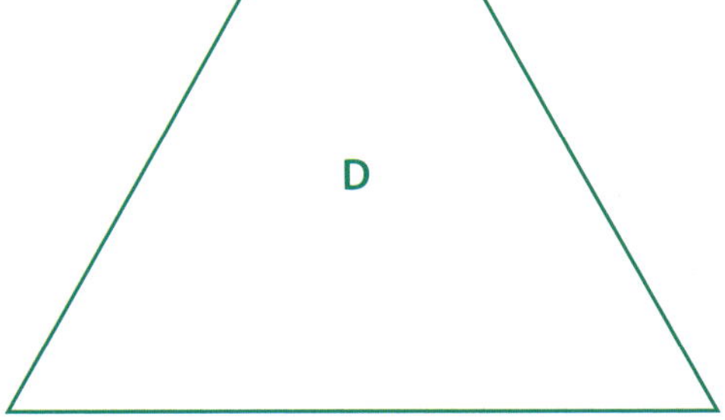

Using simple squares and rectangles, this geometric plaid wall hanging is quick to assemble and very eye-catching.

GEOMETRIC PLAID

Design by Staci Wendland

Finished Wall Hanging Size: 20$^1/_2$" x 20$^1/_2$" (52 cm x 52 cm)

SHOPPING LIST

Yardage is based on 43"/44" (109 cm/112 cm) wide fabric with a usable width of 40" (102 cm).

- ☐ 3" x 3" (8 cm x 8 cm) scrap of white solid fabric
- ☐ $^1/_4$ yard (23 cm) dark gray solid fabric (includes binding)
- ☐ $^1/_4$ yard (23 cm) medium gray solid fabric
- ☐ $^1/_8$ yard (11 cm) light gray solid fabric
- ☐ $^5/_8$ yard (57 cm) turquoise print fabric
- ☐ $^3/_4$ yard (69 cm) of fabric for backing

You will also need:

- ☐ 22" x 22" (56 cm x 56 cm) piece of batting

CUTTING THE PIECES

*Follow **Rotary Cutting**, page 55, to cut fabric. Cut all strips from the selvage-to-selvage width of the fabric. All measurements include $^1/_4$" seam allowances.*

From white fabric:

- Cut 2 strips 1" wide. From these strips, cut:
  - 4 **A** squares 1" x 1".

From dark gray fabric:

- Cut 1 strip 1$^1/_2$" wide. From this strip, cut:
  - 16 **B** squares 1$^1/_2$" x 1$^1/_2$".
- Cut 3 **binding strips** 2" wide.

From medium gray fabric:

- Cut 4 strips 1$^1/_2$" wide. From these strips, cut:
  - 8 **C** strips 1$^1/_2$" x 12".
  - 8 **D** squares 1$^1/_2$" x 1$^1/_2$".
  - 8 **E** strips 1$^1/_2$" x 3".

From light gray fabric:

- Cut 3 strips 1" wide. From these strips, cut:
  - 4 **F** strips 1" x 13".
  - 4 **G** strips 1" x 4".
  - 4 **H** strips 1" x 3$^1/_2$".

From turquoise print fabric:

- Cut 1 strip 12" wide. From this strip, cut:
  - 1 **I** square 12" x 12".
- Cut 1 strip 1$^1/_2$" wide. From this strip, cut:
  - 2 **J** strips 1$^1/_2$" x 12".
- Cut 1 strip 3" wide. From this strip, cut:
  - 2 **K** strips 3" x 12".
  - 1 **L** square 3" x 3".
  - 2 **M** strips 1$^1/_2$" x 3".
  - 1 **N** square 1$^1/_2$" x 1$^1/_2$".

From backing fabric:

- Cut **backing** 22" x 22".

THE PRIVATE LIFE OF A MASTERPIECE

ASSEMBLING THE WALL HANGING TOP

*Follow **Machine Piecing**, page 56, and **Pressing**, page 58, to make wall hanging top. Use 1/4" seam allowances throughout. Press seam allowances in opposite direction for each adjoining seam.*

1. Refer to **Wall Hanging Top Diagram** to lay pieces out, dividing the design into five sections.

2. To create Section 1, sew upper and lower pieces together into rows. Sew rows together side by side.

3. To create Section 2, sew pieces together into a row.

4. To create Section 3, sew upper and lower pieces together into rows. Sew rows together side by side.

5. To create Section 4, sew pieces together into a row.

6. To create Section 5, sew upper and lower pieces together into rows. Sew rows together side by side.

7. Sew all sections together in numerical order.

COMPLETING THE WALL HANGING

1. Follow **Quilting**, page 58, to mark, layer, and quilt as desired. Wall hanging shown is quilted in a grid.

2. Follow **Making a Hanging Sleeve**, page 60, if a hanging sleeve is desired.

3. Use **binding strips** and follow **Making Straight Grain Binding**, page 61, to make binding. Follow **Attaching Binding with Mitered Corners**, page 61, to bind wall hanging.

Wall Hanging Top Diagram

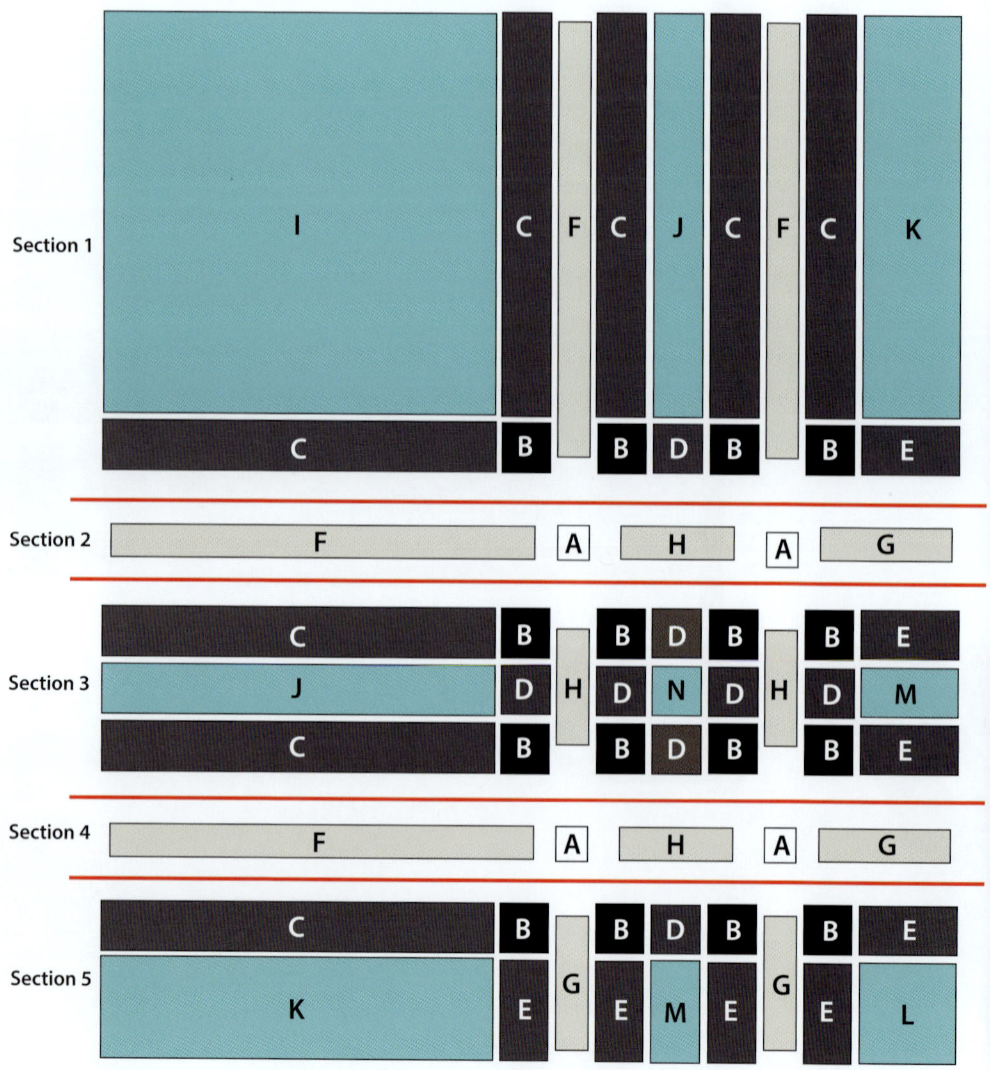

This bold, modern wall hanging is beginner-friendly and can be made quickly and easily using leftover precut 5" squares.

ADVENTURE AWAITS

Design by Shelly Morgan

Finished Wall Hanging Size: 22 1/2" x 40 1/2" (57 cm x 103 cm)

SHOPPING LIST

Yardage is based on 43"/44" (109 cm/112 cm) wide fabric with a usable width of 40" (102 cm).

- ☐ 1 1/4 yds (1.1 m) of white solid fabric
- ☐ 1/4 yd (23 cm) of dark yellow solid fabric
- ☐ 1/8 yd (11 cm) of light yellow solid fabric
- ☐ 1/4 yd (23 cm) ***each*** of 5 assorted color solid fabrics
- ☐ 1 3/4 yds (1.6 m) of fabric for backing
- ☐ 3/8 yd (34 cm) of fabric for binding

You will also need:

- ☐ 30 1/2" x 48 1/2" (77 cm x 123 cm) piece of batting
- ☐ water-soluble fabric marking pen

CUTTING THE PIECES

Follow ***Rotary Cutting****, page 55, to cut fabric. Cut all strips from the selvage-to-selvage width of the fabric. All measurements include 1/4" seam allowances.*

From white solid fabric:

- Cut 5 strips 5" wide. From these strips, cut 38 **large squares** 5" x 5".
- Cut 1 strip 5" wide. From this strip, cut 4 **rectangles** 2 3/4" x 5".
  - From remaining strip, cut 1 strip 2 3/4" wide. From this strip, cut 4 **small squares** 2 3/4" x 2 3/4".
- Cut 4 **binding strips** 2 1/4" wide.

From dark yellow solid fabric:

- Cut 1 strip 5" wide. From this strip, cut 4 **large squares** 5" x 5".

From light yellow solid fabric:

- Cut 1 strip 2 3/4" wide. From this strip, cut 8 **small squares** 2 3/4" x 2 3/4".

From *each* of 5 assorted fabrics:

- Cut 1 strip 5" wide. From this strip, cut 5 **large squares** 5" x 5".

MAKING THE UNITS

Follow ***Machine Piecing****, page 56, and* ***Pressing****, page 58, to make wall hanging top. Use 1/4" seam allowances throughout.*

Unit A

1. Using water-soluble marking pen, draw a diagonal line on the wrong side of one light yellow **small square (Fig. 1)**.

2. Place the small square on the end of one **rectangle** and stitch on the drawn line **(Fig. 2)**. Trim seam allowance to 1/4" **(Fig. 3)**. Open and press **(Fig. 4)**. Trim dog ears. This is one half of Unit A.

Fig. 1

Fig. 2

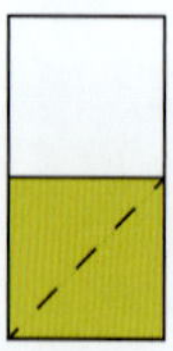

Fig. 3

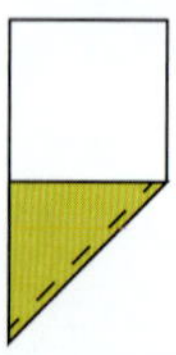

Fig. 4

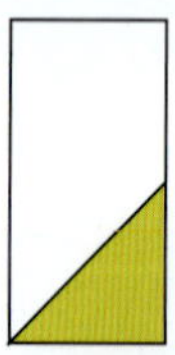

3. Repeat Steps 1-2, sewing diagonally in the opposite direction.

4. Sew units together along one long edge **(Fig. 5)** to make **Unit A**; press. Make a total of 2 Unit A's.

Fig. 5

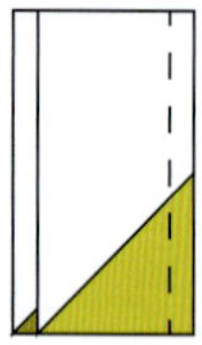

Unit A (make 2)

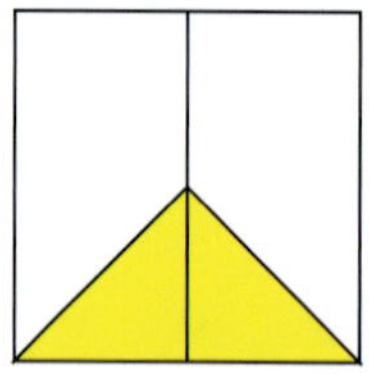

Unit B

1. Draw a diagonal line on the **wrong** side of one light yellow **small square (Fig. 6)**.

2. Place the light yellow small square on one corner of one white **large square** and stitch on the drawn line **(Fig. 7)**. Trim seam allowance to 1/4" **(Fig. 8)**. Open and press **(Fig. 9)**. Trim dog ears.

Fig. 6

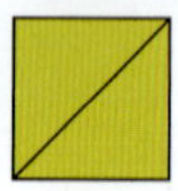

Fig. 7

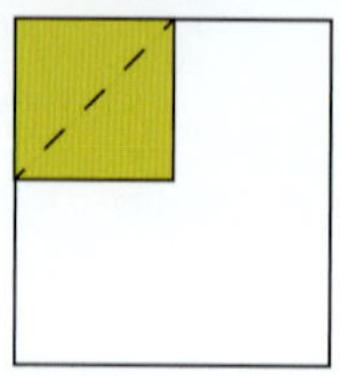

Fig. 8

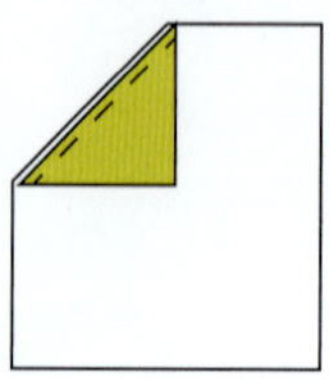

Fig. 9

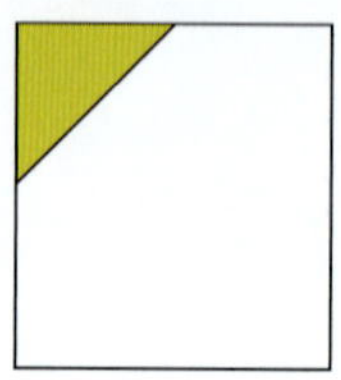

3. Repeat Steps 1-2 to sew another light yellow **small square** to the adjacent corner of the **large square** to make **Unit B**. Make a total of 2 Unit B's.

Unit B (make 2)

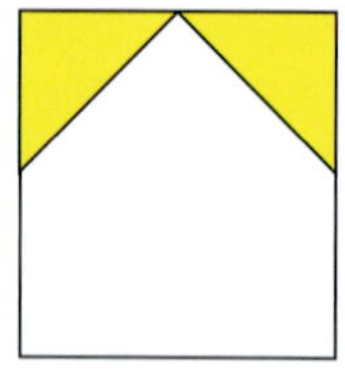

Unit C

1. Draw a diagonal line on the **wrong** side of one white **small square (Fig. 10)**.

2. Place white small square on one corner of one dark yellow **large square** and stitch on the drawn line **(Fig. 11)**. Trim seam allowance to 1/4" **(Fig. 12)**. Open and press **(Fig. 13)**. Trim dog ears.

Fig. 10

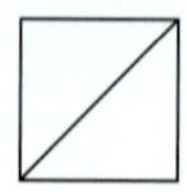

Fig. 11

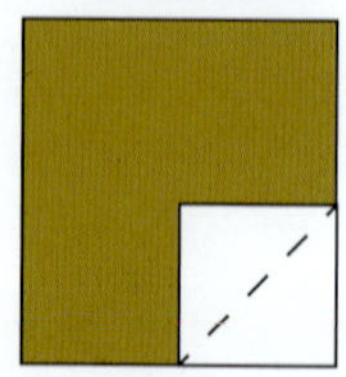

Fig. 12

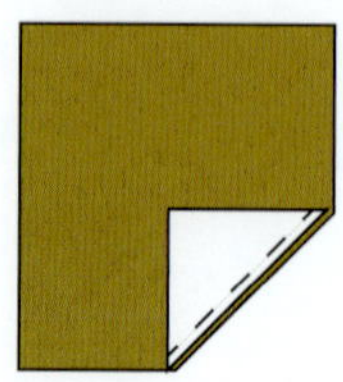

Fig. 13

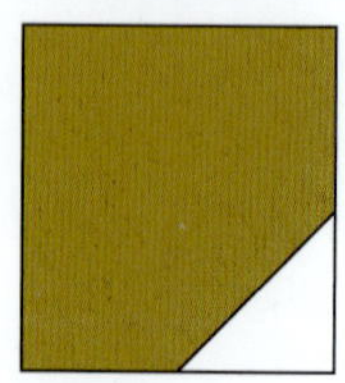

3. Draw a diagonal line on the **wrong** side of unit just made **(Fig. 14)**.

4. Place the unit on top of one white **large square** and stitch on the drawn line **(Fig. 15)**. Trim seam allowance to 1/4" **(Fig. 16)**. Open and press to make **Unit C**. Trim dog ears. Make a total of 4 Unit C's.

Fig. 14

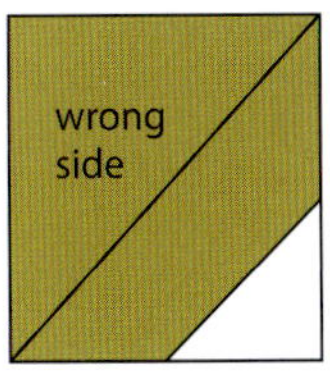

Fig. 15

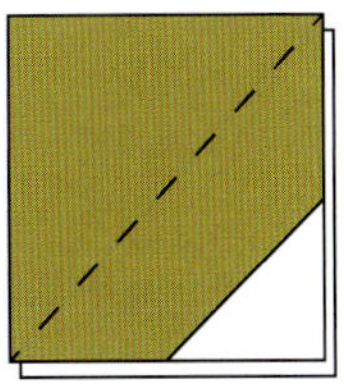

Fig. 16

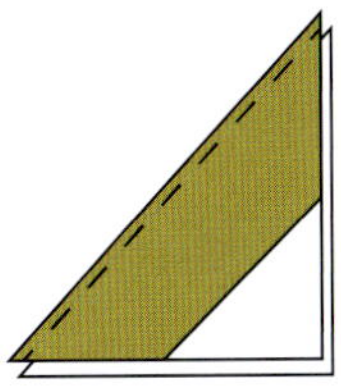

Unit C (make 4)

ASSEMBLING THE WALL HANGING TOP

*Refer to **Wall Hanging Top Diagram** to assemble wall hanging top.*

1. Sew Units and large squares together in rows as shown.

2. Show rows together to make wall hanging top.

COMPLETING THE WALL HANGING

1. Follow **Quilting**, page 58, to mark, layer, and quilt as desired. Wall hanging shown is quilted in a 1" grid.

2. Follow **Making a Hanging Sleeve**, page 60, if a hanging sleeve is desired.

3. Use **binding strips** and follow **Making Straight Grain Binding**, page 61, to make binding. Follow **Attaching Binding with Mitered Corners**, page 61, to bind wall hanging.

Wall Hanging Top Diagram

This modern take on a traditional Courthouse Steps block will be the focal point of any room you place it in.

MODERN GOD'S EYE

Design by Cindy and Sandy of Gray Barn Designs

Finished Wall Hanging Size: 30" x 54" (76 cm x 137 cm)
Finished Block A Size: 24" x 24" (61 cm x 61 cm)
Finished Block B Size: 24" x 12" (61 cm x 30 cm)

SHOPPING LIST

Yardage is based on 43"/44" (109 cm/112 cm) wide fabric with a usable width of 40" (102 cm). Fat quarters are approximately 22" x 18" (56 cm x 46 cm).

- ☐ 1 yd (91 cm) of navy blue solid fabric
- ☐ 1/4 yd (23 cm) of teal solid fabric
- ☐ 3/4 yd (69 cm) of gold solid fabric
- ☐ 7/8 yd (80 cm) of white solid fabric
- ☐ 1 3/4 yds (1.6 m) of fabric for backing

You will also need:

- ☐ 38" x 62" (97 cm x 157 cm) piece of batting

CUTTING THE PIECES

*Follow **Rotary Cutting**, page 55, to cut fabric. Cut all strips from the selvage-to-selvage width of the fabric. Borders are cut exact length. All measurements include 1/4" seam allowances.*

From navy blue solid fabric:

- Cut 5 strips 3 1/4" wide. From these strips, cut 2 **borders** 3 1/4" x 24 1/2". Piece remaining strips together and cut 2 borders 3 1/4" x 54".
- Cut 5 **binding strips** 2 1/4" wide.

From teal solid fabric:

- Cut 4 **strips** 1 1/2" wide (Block A).
- Cut one 2 1/2" x 2 1/2" **square** (Block A).

From gold solid fabric:

- Cut 16 strips 1 1/2" wide (Blocks A & B).

From white solid fabric:

- Cut 18 strips 1 1/2" wide (Blocks A & B).

From backing fabric:

- Cut 1 **backing** 38" x 62".

Sub-cut the teal, gold, and white width of fabric strips into the pieces listed in the charts below.

Tip: *Use post-it notes to help you keep track of each rectangle and strip as you cut them out. You can easily grab the size and color you need without any guess work!*

Cutting Instructions for Block A (make one of Block A)

	From Teal	From Gold	From White
2½" x 2½"	-	-	-
1½" x 2½"	-	2	-
1½" x 4½"	-	2	2
1½" x 6½"	-	2	2
1½" x 8½"	-	2	2
1½" x 10½"	-	2	2
1½" x 12½"	-	2	2
1½" x 14½"	-	2	2
1½" x 16½"	-	2	2
1½" x 18½"	-	2	2
1½" x 20½"	-	2	2
1½" x 22½"	2	-	2
1½" x 24½"	2	-	-

Cutting Instructions for Block B (make two of Block B)

	From Gold	From White
1½" x 2½"	6	2
1½" x 3½"	-	4
1½" x 4½"	4	2
1½" x 5½"	-	4
1½" x 6½"	6	-
1½" x 7½"	-	4
1½" x 8½"	4	2
1½" x 9½"	-	4
1½" x 10½"	6	-
1½" x 11½"	-	4
1½" x 12½"	4	2
1½" x 14½"	2	-
1½" x 16½"	-	2
1½" x 18½"	2	-
1½" x 20½"	-	2
1½" x 22½"	2	-

ASSEMBLING THE BLOCKS

*Follow **Machine Piecing**, page 56, to make wall hanging top. Use ¼" seam allowances throughout. Press all seams **open** unless otherwise indicated. Before pressing the seams open, gently press the seam along the stitching line. This helps "set" the seam and helps keep the seamline straight after being pressed open.*

Block A:

1. Sew one gold 1½" x 2½" rectangle to each side of the teal 2½" square to make **Unit 1**.

Unit 1

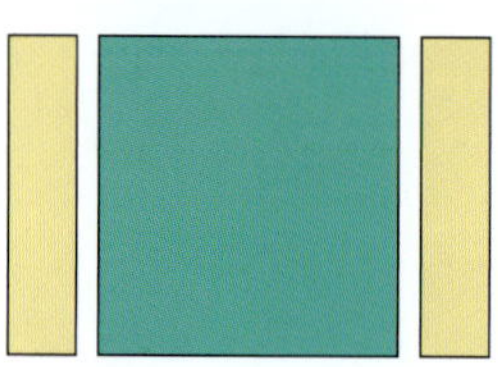

2. Sew one gold 1½" x 4½" rectangle to the top and to the bottom of Unit 1 to make **Unit 2**.

Unit 2

3. Sew one white 1½" x 4½" rectangle to each side of Unit 2 to make **Unit 3**.

Unit 3

4. Sew one white 1½" x 6½" rectangle to the top and to the bottom of Unit 3 to make **Unit 4**.

Unit 4

5. Sew one gold 1½" x 6½" rectangle to each side of Unit 4 to make **Unit 5**.

Unit 5

6. Referring to **Fig. 1**, continue sewing gold, white and teal rectangles and strips as indicated to make **Block A**. Block A should measure 24½" x 24½".

Fig. 1

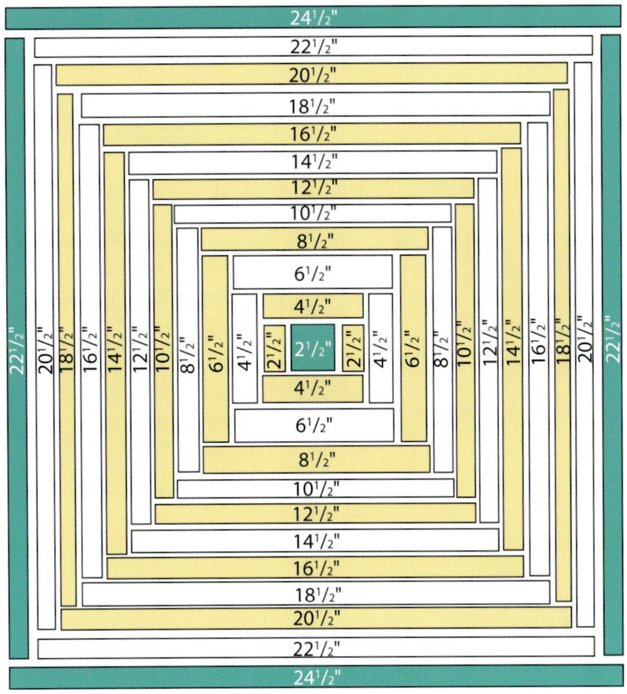

Block A

Block B:

1. Sew one gold 1 1/2" x 2 1/2" rectangle to each side of a white 1 1/2" x 2 1/2" rectangle to make **Unit 6**.

Unit 6

2. Sew one gold 1 1/2" x 2 1/2" rectangle to the top and to the bottom of Unit 6 to make **Unit 7**.

Unit 7

3. Sew one white 1 1/2" x 4 1/2" rectangle to the right of Unit 7 to make **Unit 8**.

Unit 8

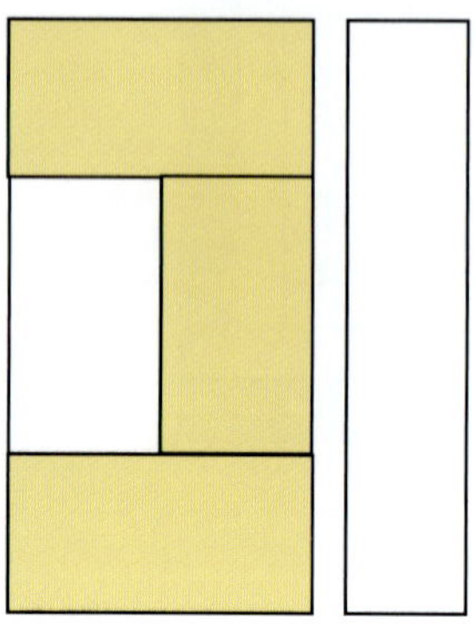

4. Sew one white 1 1/2" x 3 1/2" rectangle to the top and to the bottom of Unit 8 to make **Unit 9**.

Unit 9

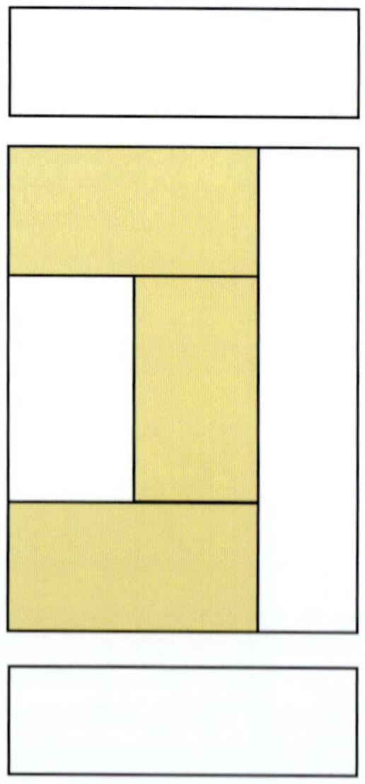

5. Sew one gold 1 1/2" x 6 1/2" rectangle to the right of Unit 9 to make **Unit 10**.

Unit 10

6. Referring to **Fig. 2**, continue sewing gold and white rectangles and strips as indicated to make **Block B**. Block B should measure 24 1/2" x 12 1/2". Repeat to make a total of two Block B's.

Fig. 2

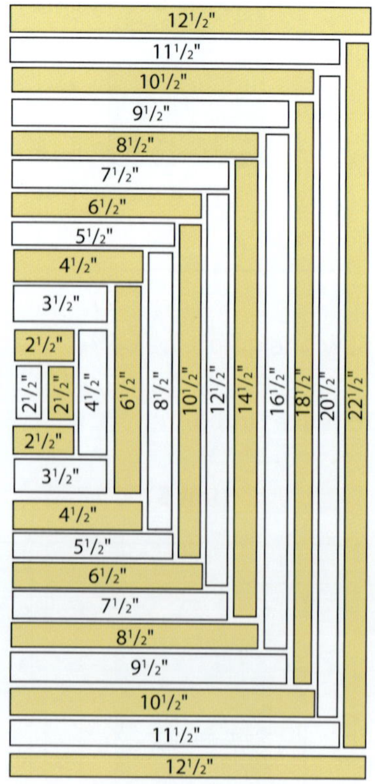

Block B (make 2)

ASSEMBLING THE WALL HANGING TOP

*Refer to **Wall Hanging Top Diagram** to assemble wall hanging.*

1. Sew the wall hanging blocks together to make **Unit 11**.

2. Sew $3^1/_4$" x $24^1/_2$" navy borders to each side of the wall hanging.

3. Refer to **Wall Hanging Top Diagram** to sew the $3^1/_4$" x 54" navy borders to the top and to the bottom.

Unit 11

Wall Hanging Top Diagram

Completing the Wall Hanging

1. Follow **Quilting**, page 58, to mark, layer, and quilt as desired. Wall hanging shown is machine quilted with an all-over meandering pattern.

2. Follow **Making a Hanging Sleeve**, page 60, if a hanging sleeve is desired.

3. Use **binding strips** and follow **Making Straight Grain Binding**, page 61, to make binding.

This quick, easy wall hanging made from squares is a great beginner project that makes a dramatic artistic statement. And there's no binding!

MODERN MOUNTAIN

Design by Staci Wendland

Finished Wall Hanging Size: 21" x 21" (53 cm x 53 cm)

SHOPPING LIST

Yardage is based on 43"/44" 109 cm/112 cm wide fabric with a usable width of 40" 102 cm .

- ☐ 1/8 yd (11 cm) ***each*** of 6 gray cotton fabrics in shades graduating from light to dark
- ☐ 1/8 yd (11 cm) ***each*** of 5 blue cotton fabric in shades graduating from light to dark
- ☐ 5/8 yd (57 cm) of fabric for backing

You will also need:

- ☐ 22" x 22" (56 cm x 56 cm) piece of fusible fleece

CUTTING THE PIECES

*Follow **Rotary Cutting**, page 55, to cut fabric. Cut all strips from the selvage-to-selvage width of the fabric. All measurements include 1/4" seam allowances.*

From gray cotton fabric #1 (lightest):
- Cut 2 squares **A** 4" x 4".

From gray cotton fabric #2:
- Cut 2 squares **B** 4" x 4".

From gray cotton fabric #3:
- Cut 2 squares **C** 4" x 4".

From gray cotton fabric #4:
- Cut 1 square **D** 4" x 4".

From gray cotton fabric #5:
- Cut 2 squares **E** 4" x 4".

From gray cotton fabric #6 (darkest):
- Cut 2 squares **F** 4" x 4".

From blue cotton fabric #1 (lightest):
- Cut 1 square **G** 4" x 4".

From blue cotton fabric #2:
- Cut 2 squares **H** 4" x 4".

From blue cotton fabric #3:
- Cut 3 squares **I** 4" x 4".

From blue cotton fabric #4:
- Cut 2 squares **J** 4" x 4".

From blue cotton fabric #5 (darkest):
- Cut 1 square **K** 4" x 4".

From fabric for backing:
- Cut 1 square 22" x 22".

ASSEMBLING THE WALL HANGING TOP

Refer to ***Wall Hanging Top Diagram*** *to assemble wall hanging top. Use $^{1}/_{4}$" seam allowances throughout. Backstitch at beginning and ending of each seam.*

1. Lay out the **squares** as shown **Fig. 1** .
2. Stitch each horizontal section of squares together to create Rows 2-5 **(Fig. 2)**.
3. Center the top square over the second square in Row 2, with right sides together, and stitch. Press the seam allowances toward the bottom.
4. Matching seamlines, stitch Row 2 and Row 3 together. Press the seam allowances toward the bottom.
5. Starting and stopping $^{1}/_{4}$" from the edge of Row 3, match seamlines and sew Row 3 To Row 4. Press the seam allowances toward the top.
6. Sew Row 5 to Row 4 in the same manner. Press the seam allowances toward the bottom.
7. Center the final square over the second square on Row 5 and stitch. Press the seam allowances toward the top.

Fig. 1

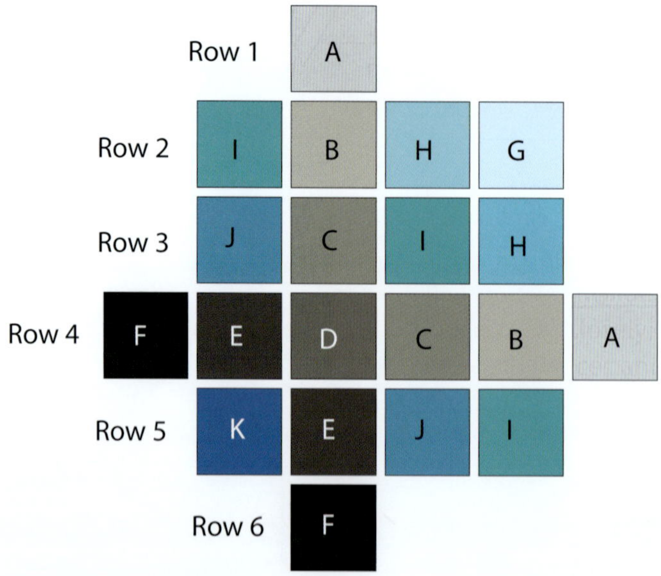

Fig. 2

COMPLETING THE WALL HANGING

1. Fuse the wall hanging top to the fusible fleece. Trim the fleece even with the wall hanging top.

2. Matching right sides, place the wall hanging top on the backing. Trim the backing to match the wall hanging top. Pin the layers together.

3. Stitch around the edge, leaving a 5" opening on one edge. Clip corners and turn right side out. Push out the corners.

4. Press the wall hanging, turning the opening edges 1/4" to inside.

5. Stitch around the wall hanging top close to the edge.

6. Follow **Quilting**, page 58, quilt as desired.

Wall Hanging Top Diagram

This bright and fun quilted wall hanging would look great in any room and in any color scheme, including monochromatic.

MOSAIC

Design by Sonya Blackstone

Finished Wall Hanging Size: 35" x 33 1/4" (89 cm x 84 cm)

SHOPPING LIST

Yardage is based on 43"/44" (109 cm/112 cm) wide fabric with a usable width of 40" (102 cm).

- ☐ 3/8 yd (34 cm) ***each*** of orange and green print fabrics
- ☐ 1/4 yd (23 cm) ***each*** of yellow and blue print fabrics
- ☐ 1 1/4 yds (1.1 m) of white print fabric
- ☐ 1 1/2 yds (1.4 m) of black print fabric for backing and binding

You will also need:

- ☐ 40" x 38" (102 cm x 97 cm) piece of batting

CUTTING THE PIECES

*Follow **Rotary Cutting**, page 55, to cut fabric. Cut all strips from the selvage-to-selvage width of the fabric. All measurements include 1/4" seam allowances.*

From orange fabric:

- Cut 1 strip 2 1/4" wide. From this strip, cut 2 rectangles **D** 2 1/4" x 11".
- Cut 2 strips 2 1/4" wide. From these strips, cut 18 rectangles **J** 2 1/4" x 4" .
- Cut 1 strip 2 1/4" wide. From this strip, cut 4 squares **L** 2 1/4" x 2 1/4".

From green fabric:

- Cut 1 strip 2 1/4" wide. From this strip, cut 2 rectangles **D** 2 1/4" x 11".
- Cut 1 strip 2 1/4" wide. From this strip, cut 2 rectangles **G** 2 1/4" x 7 1/2", 2 rectangles **H** 2 1/4" x 5 3/4", and 4 squares **L** 2 1/4" x 2 1/4".
- Cut 1 strip 2 1/4" wide. From this strip, cut 10 rectangles **J** 2 1/4" x 4".

From yellow fabric:

- Cut 2 strips 2 1/4" wide. From these strips, cut 2 rectangles **G** 2 1/4" x 7 1/2", 6 rectangles **J** 2 1/4" x 4", and 2 squares **L** 2 1/4" x 2 1/4".

From blue fabric:

- Cut 1 strip 2 1/4" wide. From this strip, cut 1 rectangle **G** 2 1/4" x 7 1/2", 2 rectangles **J** 2 1/4" x 4", and 2 squares **L** 2 1/4" x 2 1/4".

From white fabric:

- Cut 2 strips 2 1/4" wide. From these strips, cut 2 rectangles **A** 2 1/4" x 35 1/2".
- Cut 4 strips 2 1/4" wide. From these strips, cut 4 rectangles **B** 2 1/4" x 26".
- Cut 2 strips 2 1/4" wide. From these strips, cut 4 rectangles **C** 2 1/4" x 12 3/4".
- Cut 2 strips 2 1/4" wide. From these strips, cut 4 rectangles **D** 2 1/4" x 11".
- Cut 2 strips 2 1/4" wide. From these strips, cut 4 rectangles **E** 2 1/4" x 10 5/8".
- Cut 1 strip 2 1/4" wide. From this strip, cut 4 rectangles **F** 2 1/4" x 9 1/4".
- Cut 1 strip 2 1/4" wide. From this strip, cut 4 rectangles **G** 2 1/4" x 7 1/2".
- Cut 1 strip 2 1/4" wide. From this strip, cut 6 rectangles **H** 2 1/4" x 5 3/4".
- Cut 1 strip 2 1/4" wide. From this strip, cut 2 rectangles **I** 2 1/4" x 5 1/4", 6 rectangles **K** 2 1/4" x 3 1/2", and 4 rectangles **M** 2 1/4" x 1 3/4".

From fabric for binding:

- Cut **backing** 40" x 38".
- Cut 5 **binding strips** 2 1/4" wide.

The REST of HER LIFE

ASSEMBLING THE WALL HANGING TOP

*Follow **Machine Piecing**, page 56, and **Pressing**, page 58, to make wall hanging top. Use 1/2" seam allowances throughout. Refer to **Wall hanging Top Diagram** to assemble wall hanging top.*

1. Sew all pieces together in horizontal rows as shown on **Wall Hanging Top Diagram.**
2. Matching seams, sew each row together from top to bottom.

COMPLETING THE WALL HANGING

1. Follow **Quilting**, page 58, to mark, layer, and quilt as desired. Wall hanging shown is stitched in the ditch between each horizontal row.
2. Follow **Making a Hanging Sleeve**, page 60, if a hanging sleeve is desired.
3. Use **binding strips** and follow **Making Straight Grain Binding**, page 61, to make binding.

Wall Hanging Top Diagram

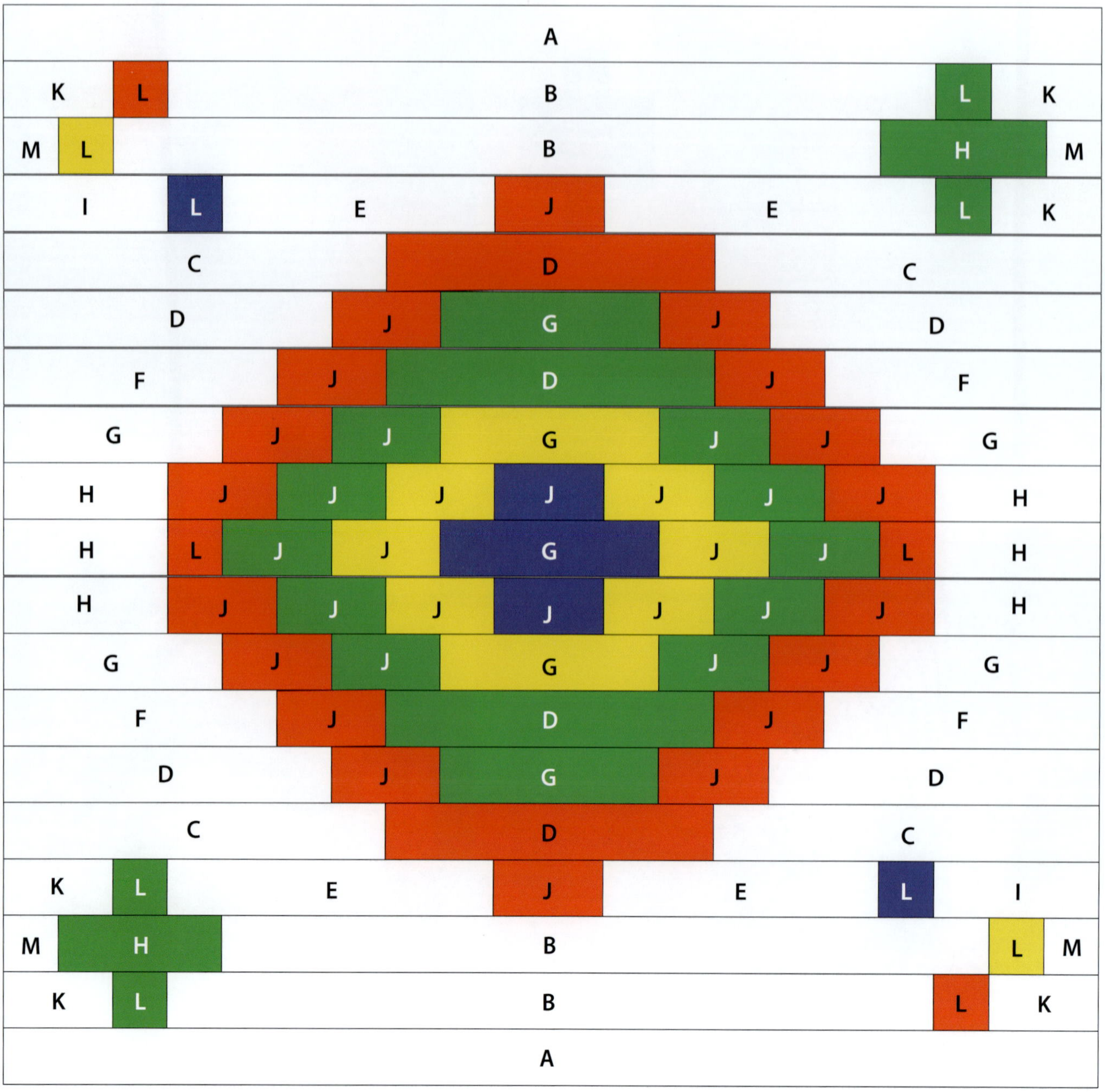

LAURA MORIARTY
The REST of HER LIFE

Majestic mountains will grace your walls with this artistic wall hanging. And it's simple to hang with wood dowels or sticks from your yard.

MOUNTAINS

Design by Alicia Steele

Finished Wall Hanging Size: approximately 56" x 34" (142 cm x 86 cm)

SHOPPING LIST

Yardage is based on 43"/44" (109 cm/112 cm) wide fabric with a usable width of 40" (102 cm).

- ☐ 1/2 yard (46 cm) ***each*** of purple, yellow, and brown solid fabrics
- ☐ 3/8 yard (34 cm) ***each*** of red, orange, and white solid fabrics
- ☐ 1 5/8 yds (1.5 m) of fabric for backing

You will also need:

- ☐ 34" x 56" (86 cm x 142 cm) piece of fusible batting
- ☐ 15 yards (13.7 m) of jute
- ☐ dowels or sticks for hanging panels

CUTTING THE PIECES

Follow ***Rotary Cutting****, page 55, to cut fabric. Cut all strips from the selvage-to-selvage width of the fabric. All measurements include 1/4" seam allowances.*

From purple solid fabric:

- Cut 2 strips 6 1/2" wide. From these strips, cut:
  - 2 **rectangles** 12 1/2" x 6½".
  - 4 **squares** 6 1/2" x 6 1/2".
  - 2 **rectangles** 6 1/2" x 2 1/2".

From yellow solid fabric:

- Cut 1 strip 6 1/2" wide. From this strip, cut:
  - 2 **squares** 6 1/2" x 6 1/2".
  - 4 **rectangles** 6 1/2" x 2 1/2".
- Cut 1 strip 2 1/2" wide. From this strip, cut:
  - 2 **rectangles** 2 1/2" x 4 1/2".
  - 4 **squares** 2 1/2" x 2 1/2".
- Cut 1 strip 2 7/8" wide. From this strip, cut:
  - 5 **squares** 2 7/8" x 2 7/8".
- Cut 1 strip 4 7/8" wide. From this strip, cut:
  - 2 **squares** 4 7/8" x 4 7/8".

From brown solid fabric:

- Cut 1 strip 6 1/2" wide. From this strip, cut:
  - 4 **rectangles** 4 1/2" x 6 1/2".
  - 2 **rectangles** 6 1/2" x 8 1/2".
- Cut 1 strip 4 7/8" wide. From this strip, cut:
  - Cut 2 **squares** 4 7/8" x 4 7/8".
- Cut 1 strip 2 7/8" wide. From this strip, cut:
  - Cut 7 **squares** 2 7/8" x 2 7/8".

From red solid fabric:

- Cut 1 strip 6 1/2" wide. From this strip, cut:
  - Cut 8 **rectangles** 6 1/2" x 4 1/2".

From orange solid fabric:

- Cut 1 strip 6 1/2" wide. From this strip, cut:
  - Cut 6 **rectangles** 6 1/2" x 4 1/2".
- Cut 1 strip 4 7/8" wide. From this strip, cut:
  - Cut 1 **squares** 4 7/8" x 4 7/8" and 2 **rectangles** 2 1/2" x 4 1/2".

From white solid fabric:

- Cut 1 strip 4 7/8" wide. From this strip, cut:
  - Cut 1 **squares** 4 7/8" x 4 7/8" and 6 **squares** 2 7/8" x 2 7/8".

From backing and batting:

- Cut 8 strips 6 1/2" wide. From these strips, cut:
  - 2 - 6 1/2" x 30 1/2".
  - 4 - 6 1/2" x 24 1/2".
  - 2 - 6 1/2" x 20 1/2".

MAKING THE HALF-SQUARE TRIANGLES

1. For the purpose of this project create half-square triangles as follows:

   Place 2 **squares** together, right sides facing each other (one of each color called for in the pattern).

   Draw a diagonal line from corner to corner. Sew 1/4" on each side of the drawn line.

   Use a rotary cutter or scissors to cut along the drawn line; press open. You now have 2 half-square triangles.

MAKING THE PANELS

Follow ***Machine Piecing****, page 56, and* ***Pressing****, page 58, to make wallhanging top. Use 1/4" seam allowances throughout.*

1. Using the 4 7/8" squares, create half-square triangles as follows:
   - 4 brown and yellow
   - 2 orange and white
2. Using the 2 7/8" squares, create half-square triangles as follows:
   - 6 brown and yellow
   - 8 white and brown
   - 4 yellow and white
3. Piece each panel together as pictured in the **Panel Diagram**. Be sure to press and square after each and every step.
4. Fuse the corresponding size batting to the wrong side of each panel. Quilt each panel as desired.
5. Cut 16 jute lengths 3" long. Fold each length in half and sew 1 loop 1" in from each corner on the top of each panel.
6. Matching right sides, place the corresponding size panel and backing together. Leaving an opening for turning along one long side, sew the panel to the backing. Turn each panel right side out; press. Sew openings closed.
7. Cut jute lengths to hang each panel. Try dip-dying portions of the jute strands for fun!

Panel Diagram

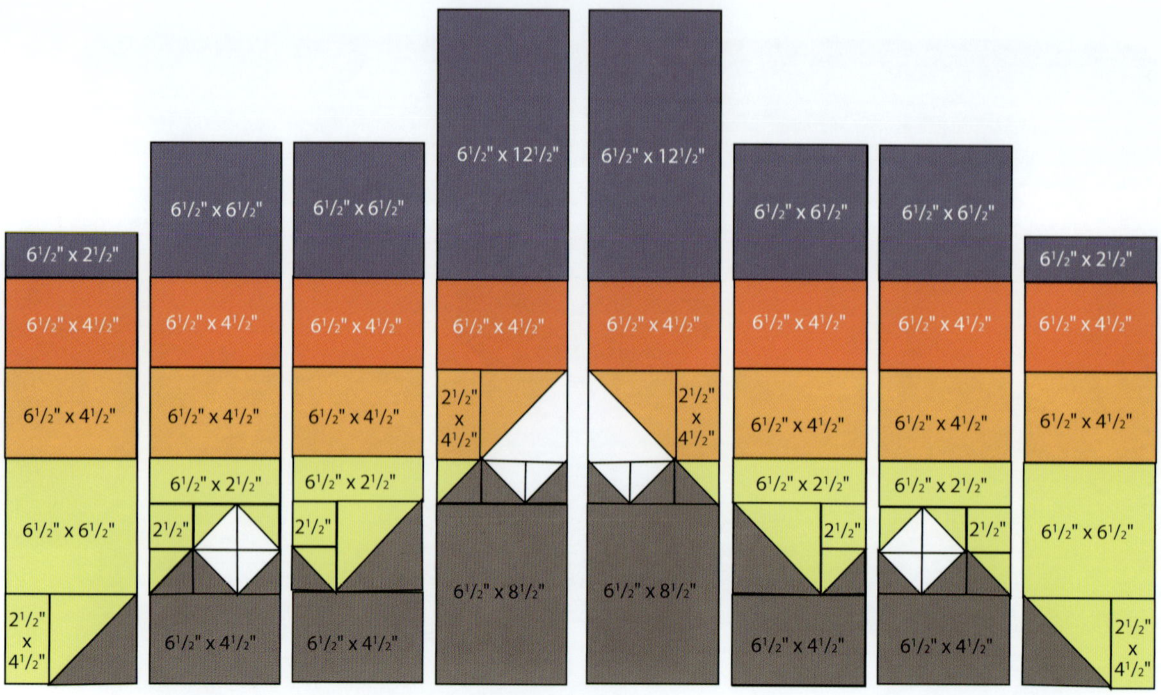

Bring some color into the space by creating this fun, simple, and unique wall hanging made from a bright jelly roll!

JELLY ROLL

Design by Katie King

Finished Wall Hanging Size: 18" x 30" (46 cm x 76 cm) (from hanging tabs to end of pom trim)
Finished Block Size: 6" x 6" (15 cm x 15 cm)

SHOPPING LIST

Yardage is based on 43"/44" (109 cm/112 cm) wide fabric with a usable width of 40" (102 cm). Jelly Rolls are 2 1/2" x approximately 40" (6 cm x 102 cm).

- ☐ 1 jelly roll or 19 strips 2 1/2" (6 cm) wide x approximately 40" (102 cm) long
- ☐ 22" x 36" (56 cm x 91 cm) piece of fabric for backing
- ☐ 22" x 36" (56 cm x 91 cm) piece of batting

You will also need:

- ☐ 5/8 yard (57 cm) of 3/4" (19 mm) yellow pom fringe trim (optional)

MAKING THE BLOCKS

Follow ***Machine Piecing****, page 56, and* ***Pressing****, page 58, to make wall hanging top. Use 1/4" seam allowances throughout.*

1. Choose 6 jelly roll strips. Trim those strips 18 1/2" long; set aside.
2. Choose 3 more jelly roll strips (that have not been cut) and sew long edges together to make a Strip Set. Cut the Strip Set into three 6 1/2" x 6½" **Blocks**.

Block (make 3 from each set of 3 jelly roll strips)

3. Repeat Step 2, using two more groups of 3 jelly roll strips to make a total of 9 Blocks.

ASSEMBLING THE WALL HANGING TOP

1. Alternating blocks, sew 3 blocks together to make a **Row**. Make 3 Rows.

2. Arrange fabric strips and Rows as shown in photo, page 37. Sew the Rows and strips together.

3. Follow **Quilting**, page 58, to mark, layer, and quilt as desired. Wall hanging shown is quilted using the straight-line method.

4. Choose a jelly roll strip and cut 3 hanging tabs 6" long. Matching right sides and long raw edges, fold 1 hanging tab in half lengthwise and sew along long raw edges. Turn the hanging tab right side out. Repeat with remaining hanging tabs. Set tabs aside.

5. Choose 3 jelly roll strips and follow **Making Straight Grain Binding**, page 61, to make binding.

6. Follow **Attaching Binding with Mitered Corners**, page 61, Steps 1 - 13 to attach binding to front of wall hanging. Fold the tabs in half and pin them at 2" from each top corner and at the center top **(Fig. 1)**. Follow **Attaching Binding with Mitered Corners**, Steps 14 - 15 to complete attaching binding.

7. Cut a piece of trim and hand sew it to the bottom of the wall hanging.

Fig. 1

Katie King would like to thank Robert Kaufman Fabrics for providing these beautiful Palm Canyon fabrics.

Believed to have the power to catch all of a person's dreams - good and bad - this dream catcher is a contemporary take on the traditional.

DREAM CATCHER

Design by Carolina Moore

Finished Wall Hanging Size: 23" x 43" (58 cm x 109 cm) including fringe

SHOPPING LIST

Yardage is based on 43"/44" (109 cm/112 cm) wide fabric with a usable width of 40" (102 cm).

- ☐ 1/4 yd (23 cm) ***each*** of gold, yellow, cream, blue, and dark blue solid fabric
- ☐ 7/8 yd (80 cm) of fabric for facing
- ☐ 7/8 yd (80 cm) of fabric for backing

You will also need:

- ☐ 28" x 28" (71 cm x 71 cm) piece of batting
- ☐ 23" (58 cm) diameter wooden quilting hoop
- ☐ Creative Grids® 30° Triangle Ruler
- ☐ blue embroidery floss
- ☐ large eye needle
- ☐ coordinating yarn

Carolina Moore would like to thank Art Gallery Fabrics for providing these beautiful solid fabrics.

CUTTING THE PIECES

Follow ***Rotary Cutting****, page 55, to cut fabric. Cut all strips from the selvage-to-selvage width of the fabric. All measurements include 1/4" seam allowances.*

From *each* of gold, yellow, cream, and blue solid fabrics:

- Cut 1 strip 2³/4" wide. From this strip, follow ruler manufacturer's instructions to cut 18 **equilateral triangles (Fig. 1)**.

From dark blue solid fabric:

- Cut 2 strips 2³/4" wide. From this strip, cut 24 **equilateral triangles**.

From facing fabric:

- Cut **facing** 28" x 28".

From backing fabric:

- Cut **backing** 28" x 28".

Fig. 1

ASSEMBLING THE WALL HANGING TOP

*Follow **Machine Piecing**, page 56, and **Pressing**, page 58, to make wall hanging top. Refer to **Wall Hanging Top Diagram** to assemble wall hanging top.*

Use 1/4" seam allowances throughout.

1. Piecing triangles is as easy as piecing squares. Place two **triangles**, right sides together, with all points matching. Stitch down one side. Press the seam open. Trim off the dog ears **(Fig. 2)**.

2. To attach a third triangle to the row, place the third triangle, right side up, next to the previous two **(Fig. 3)**. Then flip it over onto the stitched together set, and sew the seam. Press the seam open **(Unit 1)**.

3. Make the rows as pictured, pressing each seam open before adding the next triangle. Then stitch the rows together. Press the seams open.

4. Make 3 blue-tipped large triangle blocks **(Block A)** and 3 yellow-tipped large triangle blocks **(Block B)**.

5. Stitch the six blocks into two halves, making sure to alternate blue point and yellow point blocks **(Unit 2)**. Then stitch the two halves together to make the **Wall Hanging Top**.

Fig. 2

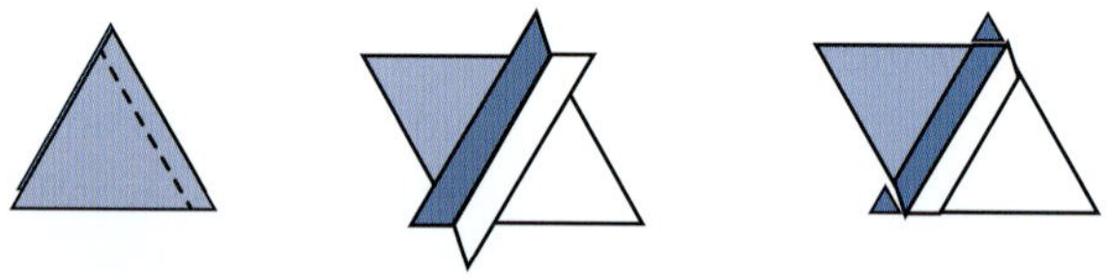

Fig. 3

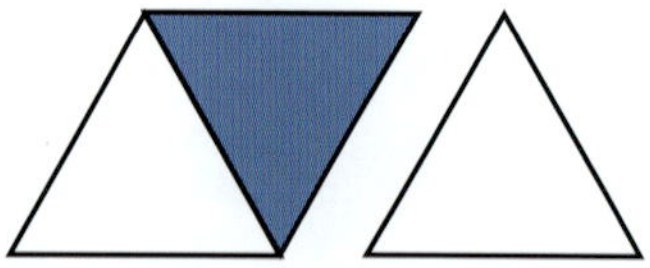

Unit 1

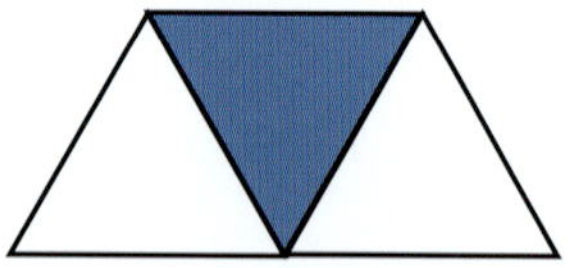

Block A (make 3)

Block B (make 3)

Unit 2

Wall Hanging Top Diagram

COMPLETING THE WALL HANGING

1. Follow **Quilting**, page 58, to mark, layer, and quilt as desired. Wall Hanging shown is quilted with a walking foot on each side of each seam. Remember that when you press seams open, you cannot "stitch in the ditch" because there is no "ditch" to quilt in. Trim the backing and batting even with the wall hanging top.

2. Place the wall hanging top on the **facing** fabric square. Trim the facing fabric to same size as wall hanging top.

3. Matching right sides and leaving an opening for turning, sew the wall hanging top and facing together along all sides. Clip corners and turn right side out; press. Sew opening closed.

4. Use embroidery floss and a large-eye needle to secure the wall hanging to the hoop. Tie off the embroidery floss on the back of the wall hanging at one of the corners. Insert the needle through the wall hanging at the corner from the back to the front. Loop the embroidery floss around the hoop, and working clockwise, secure the embroidery floss midway along the side by inserting the needle from the back to the front about $^{1}/_{4}$" from the edge. Loop around the hoop again, and repeat, securing at each corner and midway on each side until you are all the way around the wall hanging.

5. Adjust the embroidery floss as needed to center the wall hanging in the hoop. Once it is centered and the tension is even, tie off the end of the embroidery floss on the back of the wall hanging.

6. Add yarn fringe to the bottom of the hoop by tying 40" lengths of yarn to the bottom of the hoop so that the ends hang down. Once all the yarn has been tied in place, carefully trim the fringe into the desired shape and length **(Fig. 4)**.

Fig. 4

This soft and sweet wall hanging is perfect for any nursery wall. It features flannel fabrics for that extra touch of "baby". This pattern would work great in quilter's cotton and solid colors with embroidered squares.

STAGGERED

Design by Sonya Blackstone

Finished Wall Hanging Size: 36" x 42" (91 cm x 107 cm)

SHOPPING LIST

Yardage is based on 43"/44" (109 cm/112 cm) wide fabric with a usable width of 40" (102 cm).

- ☐ $^{3}/_{8}$ yd (34 cm) ***each*** of teal polka dot and small woodland animal print fabrics
- ☐ $^{1}/_{4}$ yd (23 cm) of yellow stripe fabric
- ☐ $^{1}/_{2}$ yd (46 cm) of large woodland animal print
- ☐ 2 yds (1.8 m) of star print (includes backing)
- ☐ $^{5}/_{8}$ yd (57 m) gray polka dot for sashing and border

You will also need:

- ☐ 5 yds (4.6 m) of 1" double-fold quilt bias tape for binding
- ☐ 40" x 46" (102 cm x 117 cm) piece of batting
- ☐ 20 yds (18.3 m) of gray worsted weight yarn
- ☐ $3^{1}/_{2}$" x $5^{1}/_{2}$" (9 cm x 14 cm) piece of lightweight cardboard

CUTTING THE PIECES

*Follow **Rotary Cutting**, page 55, to cut fabric. Cut all strips from the selvage-to-selvage width of the fabric. Borders are cut exact length. All measurements include $^{1}/_{4}$" seam allowances.*

From teal polka dot fabric:

- Cut 1 **H** $6^{1}/_{2}$" x $7^{1}/_{2}$".
- Cut 1 **D** $5^{1}/_{2}$" x $10^{1}/_{2}$".
- Cut 1 **O** $6^{1}/_{2}$" x $6^{1}/_{2}$".
- Cut 1 **R** $7^{1}/_{2}$" x $7^{1}/_{2}$".

From yellow stripe fabric:

- Cut 1 **A** $7^{1}/_{2}$" x $7^{1}/_{2}$".
- Cut 1 **I** $6^{1}/_{2}$" x $7^{1}/_{2}$".
- Cut 1 **P** $5^{1}/_{2}$" x $6^{1}/_{2}$".
- Cut 1 **U** $8^{1}/_{2}$" x $3^{1}/_{2}$".

From small woodland animal print fabric:

- Cut 1 **C** $5^{1}/_{2}$" x $5^{1}/_{2}$".
- Cut 1 **L** $5^{1}/_{2}$" x $8^{1}/_{2}$".
- Cut 1 **Q** $11^{1}/_{2}$" x $6^{1}/_{2}$".

From large woodland animal print fabric:

- Cut 1 **F** $8^{1}/_{2}$" x $6^{1}/_{2}$".
- Cut 1 **K** $6^{1}/_{2}$" x $9^{1}/_{2}$".
- Cut 1 **E** $12^{1}/_{2}$" x $7^{1}/_{2}$".
- Cut 1 **T** $8^{1}/_{2}$" x $12^{1}/_{2}$".
- Cut 1 **N** $6^{1}/_{2}$" x $8^{1}/_{2}$".

From star print fabric:

- Cut 1 **backing** 40" x 46".
- Cut 1 **B** $7^{1}/_{2}$" x $8^{1}/_{2}$".
- Cut 1 **G** $8^{1}/_{2}$" x $8^{1}/_{2}$".
- Cut 1 **J** $6^{1}/_{2}$" x $5^{1}/_{2}$".
- Cut 1 **V** $15^{1}/_{2}$" x $5^{1}/_{2}$".
- Cut 1 **M** $6^{1}/_{2}$" x $4^{1}/_{2}$".
- Cut 1 **S** $7^{1}/_{2}$" x $8^{1}/_{2}$".

From gray polka dot print fabric:

- Cut 5 strips $1^{1}/_{2}$" wide. From these strips, cut:
  - 3 sashings **W** $1^{1}/_{2}$" x $7^{1}/_{2}$".
  - 3 sashings **X** $1^{1}/_{2}$" x $5^{1}/_{2}$".
  - 3 sashings **Y** $1^{1}/_{2}$" x $8^{1}/_{2}$".
  - 5 sashings **Z** $1^{1}/_{2}$" x $6^{1}/_{2}$".
  - 1 sashing **AA** $1^{1}/_{2}$" x $12^{1}/_{2}$".
  - 1 sashing **BB** $1^{1}/_{2}$" x $15^{1}/_{2}$".
  - 1 sashing **CC** $1^{1}/_{2}$" x $11^{1}/_{2}$".
- Cut 2 **top/bottom borders** $2^{1}/_{4}$" x $36^{1}/_{2}$".
- Cut 2 **side borders** $2^{1}/_{4}$" x $38^{1}/_{2}$".

ASSEMBLING THE WALL HANGING TOP

*Follow **Machine Piecing**, page 56, and **Pressing**, page 58, to make wall hanging top. Use 1/4" seam allowances throughout.*

1. Referring to **Wall Hanging Top Diagram**, stitch one corresponding width **sashing** to the top of each **square** or **rectangle**, excluding top row of squares and rectangless. Example: Stitch one 7 1/2" wide sashing to top of one 7 1/2" wide square or rectangle.
2. Stitch A to B.
3. Stitch C to D.
4. Stitch AB to CD.
5. Stitch ABCD to E.
6. Stitch F to G.
7. Stitch FG to CD, lining them up at the top edge. Leave 1" unstitched at the ends of D and G for attaching L later.
8. Stitch H to I.
9. Stitch J to K.
10. Stitch HI to JK.
11. Stitch FG to HI.
12. Stitch L to the bottom of G, lining it up on the left edge.
13. Stitch L to D and E.
14. Stitch M to N.
15. Stitch O to P.
16. Stitch OP to Q.
17. Stitch MN to O and Q.
18. Stitch MOP to EL.
19. Stitch R to S.
20. Stitch T to U.
21. Stitch RS to TU.
22. Stitch V to RT.
23. Finish stitching the top of V to G, I, and K and left side of VRS to LPQ.
24. Stitch side borders first and then top and bottom borders to wall hanging top.

COMPLETING THE WALL HANGING

1. Follow **Quilting**, page 58, to mark, layer, and quilt as desired. Wall hanging shown is quilted in the ditch along the seamlines.
2. Follow **Making a Hanging Sleeve**, page 60, if a hanging sleeve is desired.
3. Use **bias tape** and follow **Attaching Binding with Mitered Corners**, page 61, using 1/2" seam allowances to bind wall hanging.

Wall Hanging Top Diagram

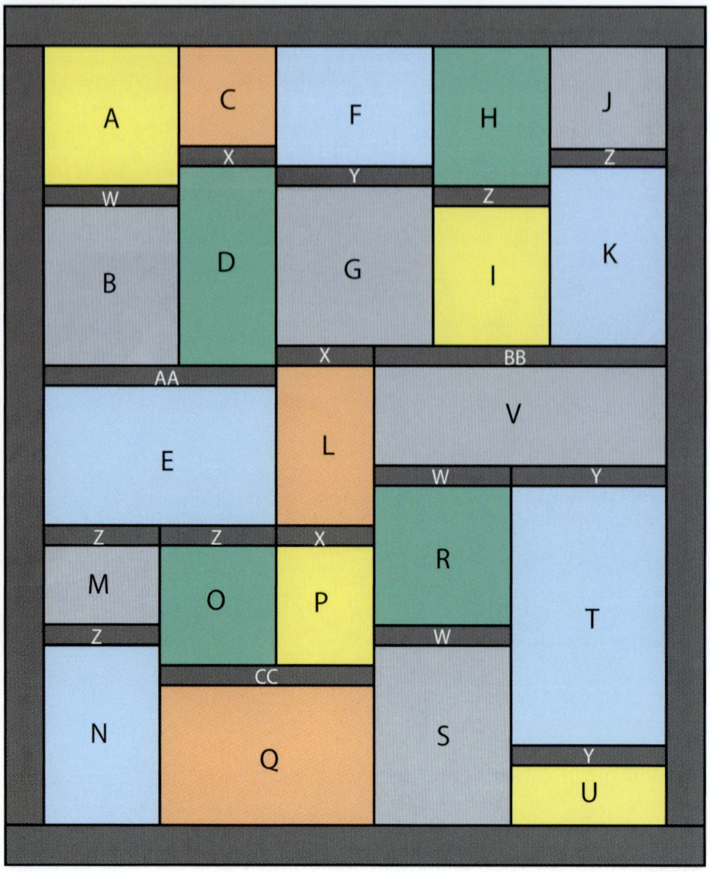

ADDING THE TASSELS

1. Cut eight 10" lengths of yarn; set aside.

2. Wrap the yarn around the cardboard in the longer direction about 50 times. Trim the yarn from the skein.

3. Slip a 10" length of yarn behind the wraps and bring it to the top of the cardboard; tie a secure knot.

4. Cut the yarn loops on the end opposite the knot **(Fig. 1)**. Remove the cardboard.

5. Holding the yarn ends together, tie a 10" yarn length around the tassel about 1$^1/_2$" below the knot **(Fig. 2)**. Trim tassel ends even.

6. Repeat Steps 2-5 to make a total of four tassels.

Fig. 1

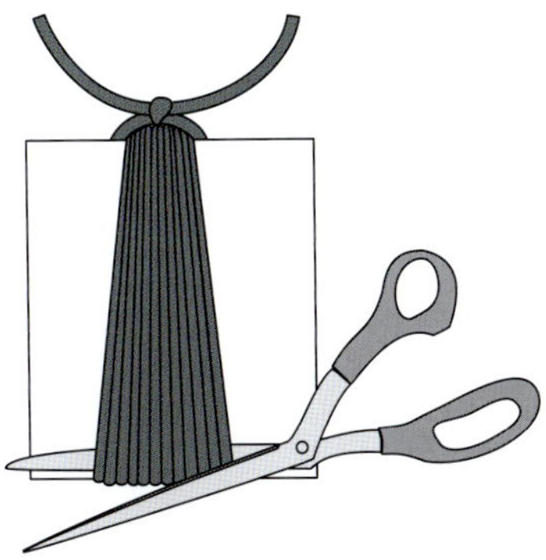

Fig. 2

This "gem" of a wall hanging is sure to bring eye-popping color to any room.

CORAL GEM

Design by Monica Curry

Finished Wall Hanging Size: 36" x 36" (91 cm x 91 cm)

SHOPPING LIST

Yardage is based on 43"/44" (109 cm/112 cm) wide fabric with a usable width of 40" (102 cm).

- ☐ $1^{3}/_{8}$ yards (1.3 m) white solid fabric
- ☐ $^{1}/_{2}$ yard (46 cm) lime solid fabric
- ☐ $^{1}/_{8}$ yard (11 cm) lavender solid fabric
- ☐ 1 yard (91 cm) green solid fabric
- ☐ $^{1}/_{4}$ yard (23 cm) orange solid fabric
- ☐ $1^{1}/_{4}$ yds (1.1 m) of fabric for backing

You will also need:

- ☐ 44" x 44" (112 cm x 112 cm) piece of batting
- ☐ template plastic
- ☐ water-soluble fabric marking pen

CUTTING THE PIECES

Follow ***Rotary Cutting****, page 55, and* ***Making and Using Templates****, page 56, to cut fabric. Cut all strips from the selvage-to-selvage width of the fabric. Borders are cut exact length. All measurements include $^{1}/_{4}$" seam allowances.*

From white solid fabric:

- Use templates to cut:
  - 4 **A4** squares.
  - 8 **A3** triangles.
  - 4 **G1** pieces.
  - 4 **G3** pieces.
  - 4 **H1** pieces.
- Cut 1 strip $12^{1}/_{2}$" wide. From this strip, cut:
  - 4 rectangles **B** $3^{1}/_{2}$" x $12^{1}/_{2}$".
  - 4 rectangles **D** $1^{3}/_{4}$" x $12^{1}/_{2}$".
- Cut 4 strips $4^{3}/_{4}$" wide. From these strips, cut:
  - 4 rectangles **E** $4^{3}/_{4}$" x $24^{1}/_{2}$".

From lime solid fabric:

- Use templates to cut:
  - 8 **A3** triangles.
  - 4 **G2** pieces.
- Cut 2 strips $2^{1}/_{4}$" wide. From these strips, cut 4 rectangles **C** $2^{1}/_{4}$" x $12^{1}/_{2}$".

From lavender solid fabric:

- Use templates to cut:
  - 4 **A2** triangles.

From green solid fabric:

- Use templates to cut:
  - 8 **A3** squares.
  - 4 **H2** pieces.
- Cut 4 strips $2^{1}/_{4}$" wide. From these strips, cut 4 rectangles **F** $2^{1}/_{4}$" x $24^{1}/_{2}$".
- Cut 4 **binding strips** $2^{1}/_{4}$" wide.

From orange solid fabric:

- Use templates to cut:
  - 1 **A1** square.
  - 8 **A3** triangles.

ASSEMBLING THE WALL HANGING TOP

*Follow **Machine Piecing**, page 56, and **Pressing**, page 58, to make wall hanging top. Use 1/4" seam allowances throughout. Refer to **Wall Hanging Top Diagram** to sew wall hanging top.*

Block A

1. Sew **A2** triangles to opposite sides of 1 **A1** square. Sew remaining **A2** triangles to remaining sides of square to make **Unit 1**.

Unit 1

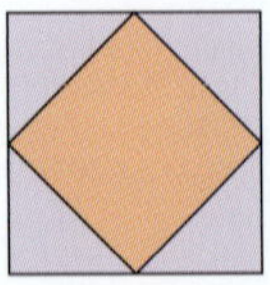

2. Sew **A3** triangles together to make 4 **Unit 2's** and 4 **Unit 3's**. Notice they are mirror images of each other.

Unit 2 (make 4)

Unit 3 (make 4)

3. Sew 1 Unit 2 and 1 Unit 3 together to make **Unit 4**. Make 4 Unit 4's.

Unit 4 (make 4)

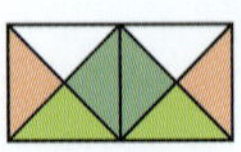

4. Sew 1 Unit 4 to top and bottom of Unit 1 to make **Unit 5**.

Unit 5

5. Sew 1 **A4** to either end of 1 Unit 4 to make **Unit 6**. Make 2 Unit 6's.

Unit 6 (make 2)

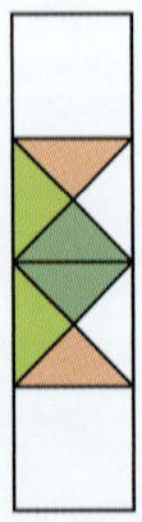

6. Sew 1 Unit 6 to either side of Unit 5 to make Block A. Block A should measure 12 1/2" x 12 1/2" including seam allowances.

Block A

BLOCK G

1. Sew pieces **G1**, **G2**, and **G3** together to make **Block G**. Make 4 Block G's.

Block G (make 4)

BLOCK H

1. Sew pieces **H1** and **H2** together to make **Block H**. Make 4 Block H's.

Block H (make 4)

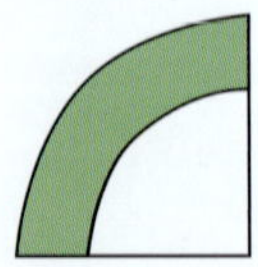

SASHINGS AND BORDERS

1. Sew pieces **B**, **C**, and **D** together to make **Sashing**. Make 4 Sashings.

Sashing (make 4)

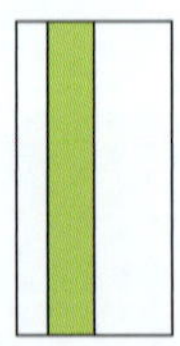

2. Sew pieces **E** and **F** together to make **Border**. Make 4 Borders.

Border (make 4)

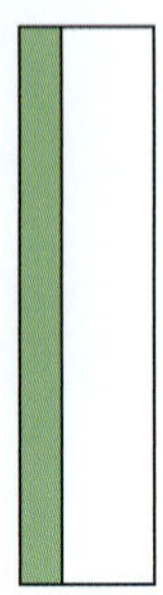

WALL HANGING TOP ASSEMBLY

1. Sew 1 Sashing to the top and bottom of Block A to make **Unit 7**.

Unit 7

2. Sew 1 Block G to the top and bottom of 1 Sashing to make **Unit 8**. Make 2 Unit 8's.

Unit 8 (make 2)

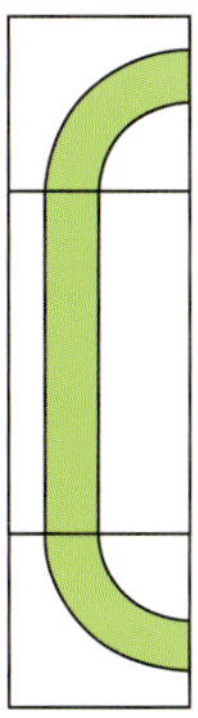

3. Sew 1 Unit 8 to each side of Unit 7 to make **Unit 9**.

Unit 9

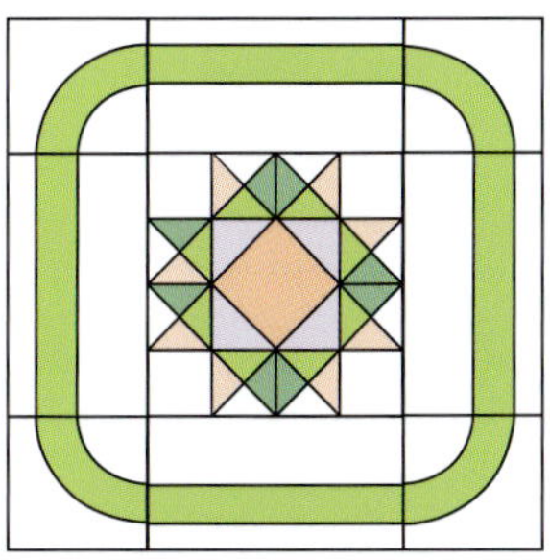

4. Sew 1 Border to top and bottom of Unit 9 to make **Unit 10**.

Unit 10

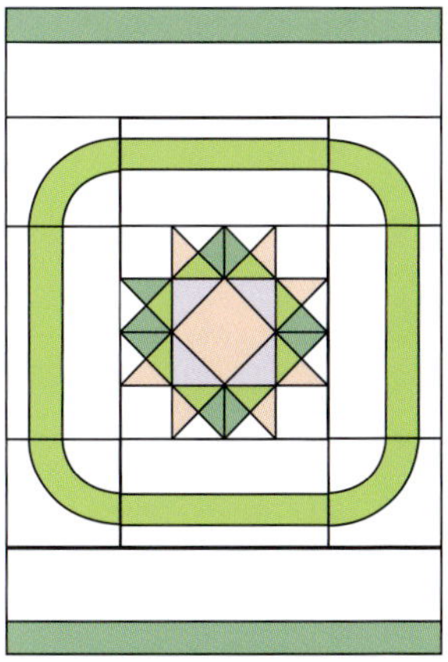

5. Sew 1 Block H to top and bottom of 1 Border to make **Unit 11**. Make 2 Unit 11's.

Unit 11 (make 2)

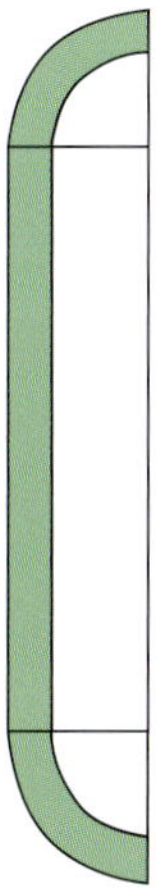

6. Sew 1 Unit 11 to each side of Unit 10 to make **Wall Hanging Top**.

COMPLETING THE WALL HANGING

1. Follow **Quilting**, page 58, to mark, layer, and quilt as desired. Wall hanging shown is quilted in diagonal lines.

2. Use the edge of a plate to mark the outer edges of the wall hanging with a water soluble marker to round the edges of the wall hanging.

3. Follow **Making a Hanging Sleeve**, page 60, if a hanging sleeve is desired.

4. Use **binding strips** and follow **Making Straight Grain Binding**, page 61, to make binding. Follow **Attaching Binding with Mitered Corners**, page 61, Steps 1 & 7-15, to bind wall hanging.

Wall Hanging Top Diagram

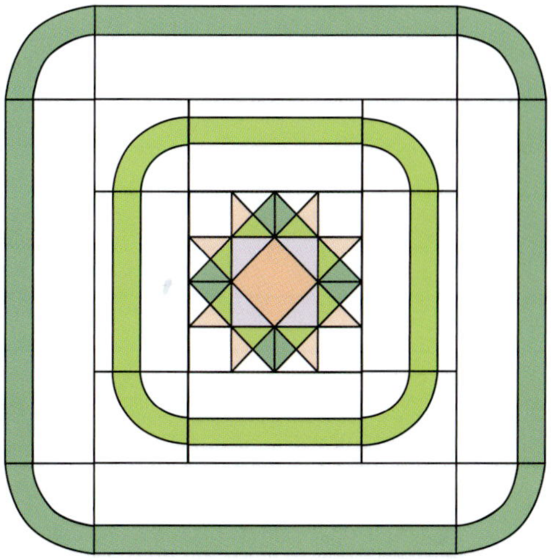

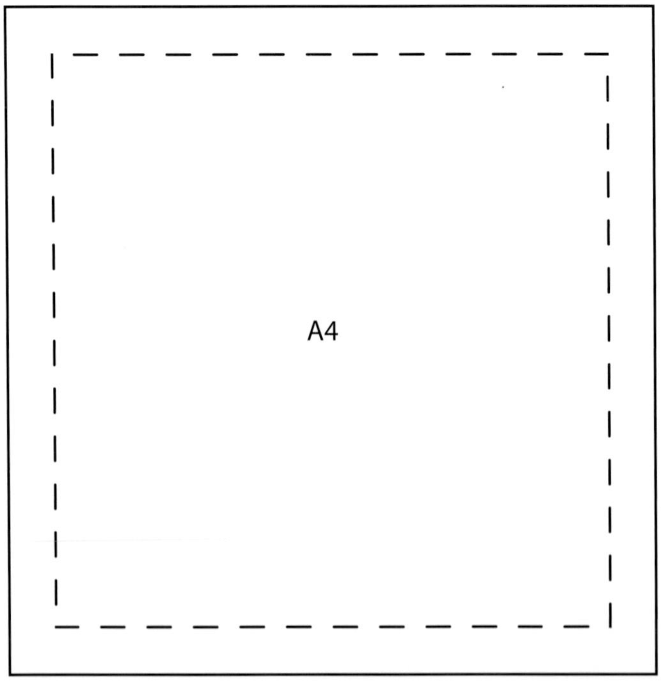
A4

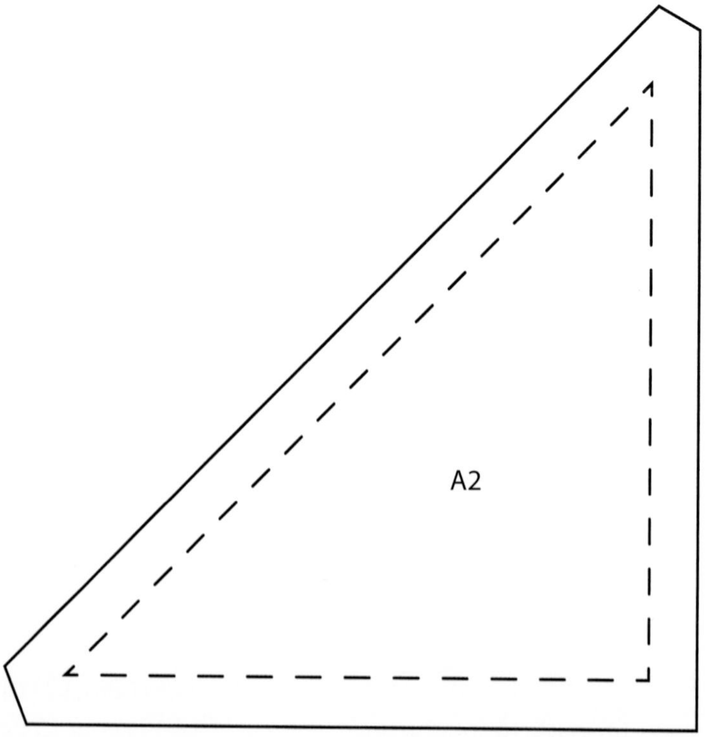
A2

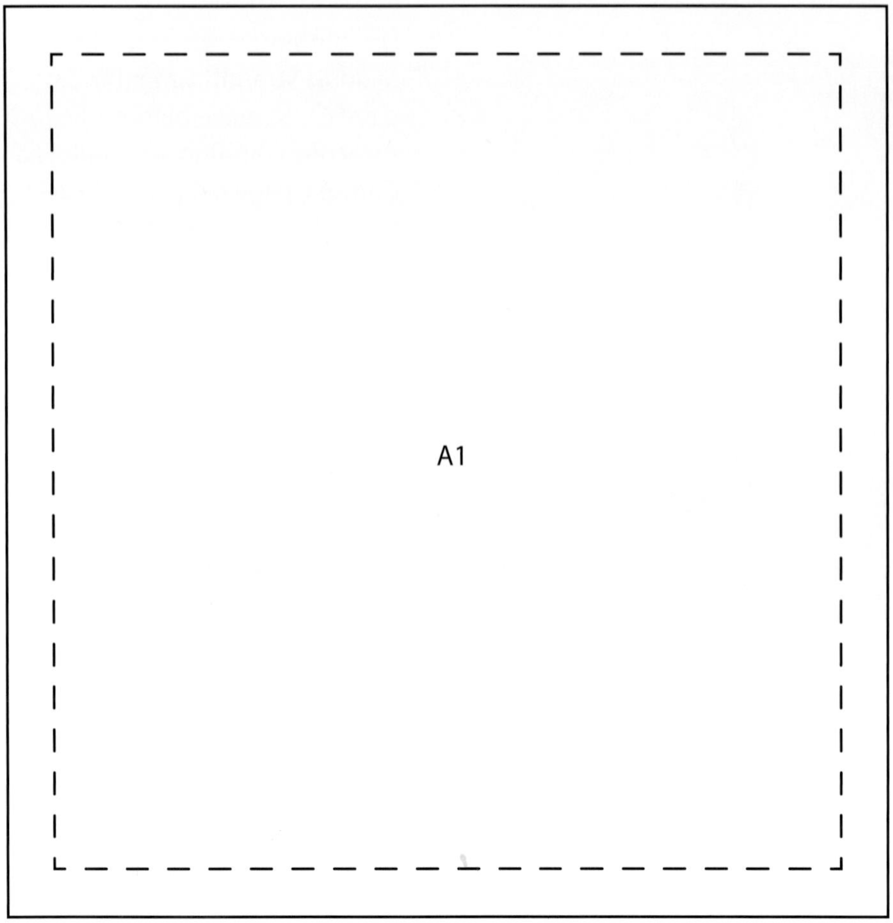
A1

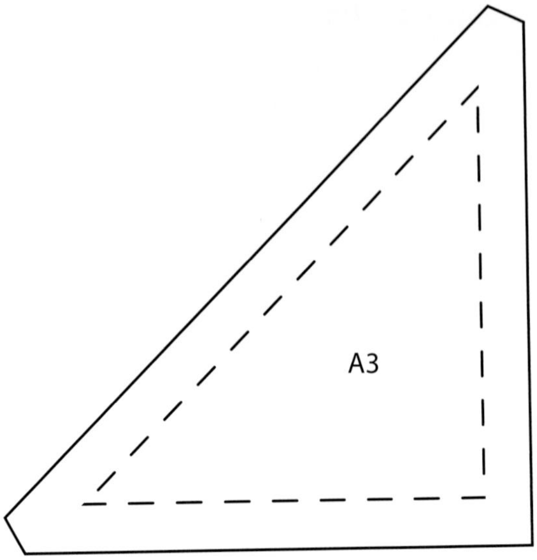
A3

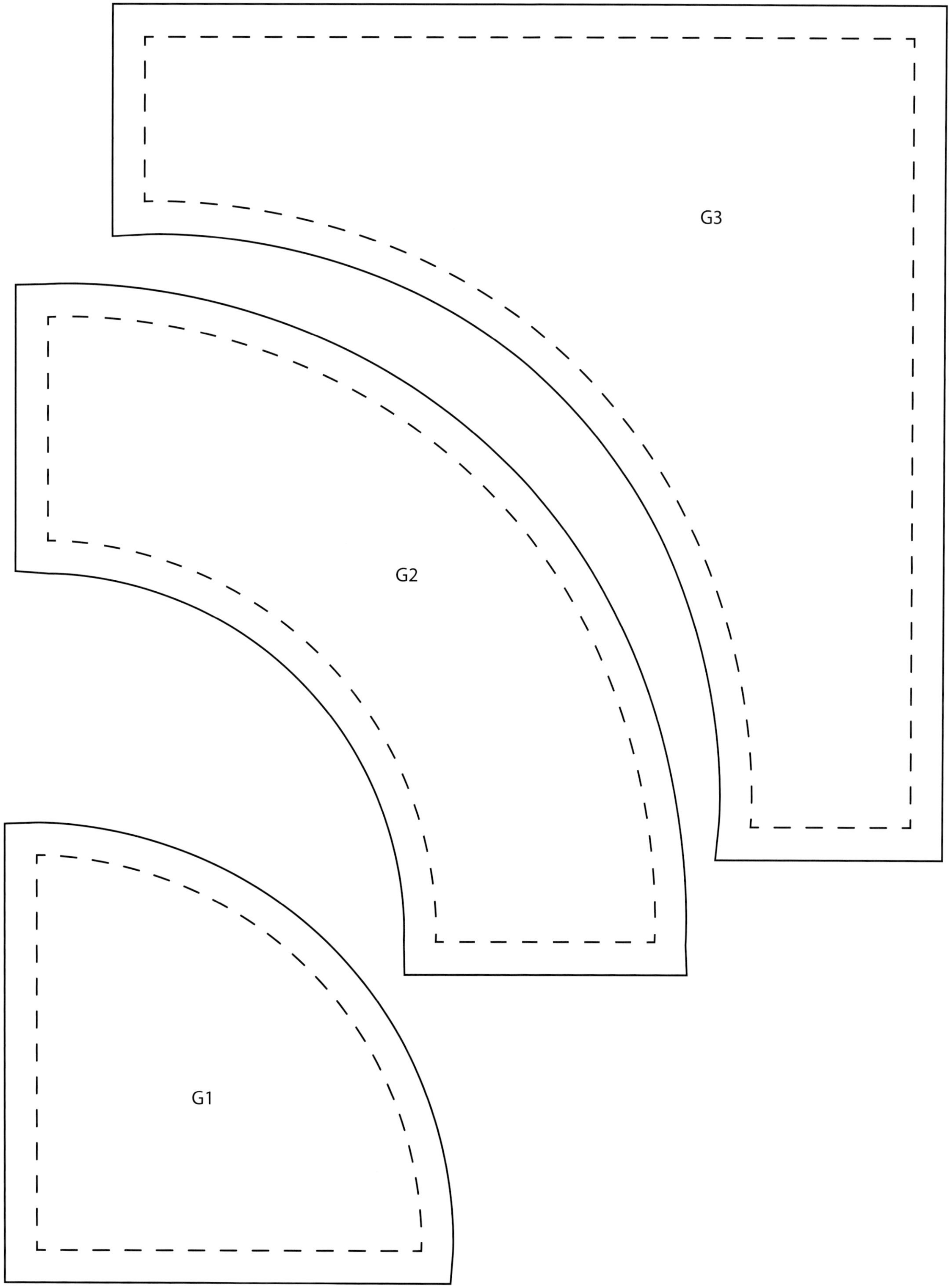
G3
G2
G1

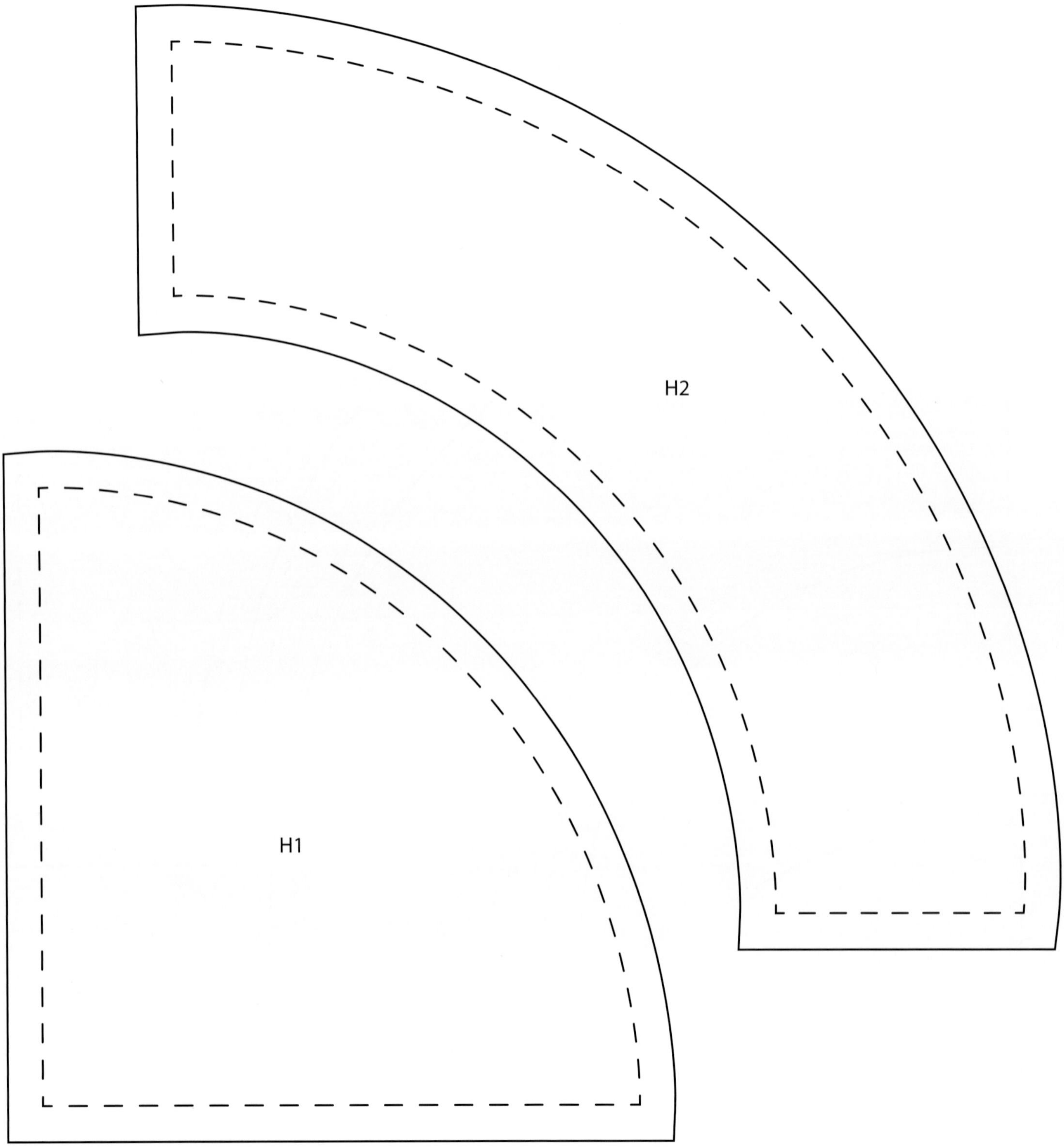
H2
H1

GENERAL INSTRUCTIONS

To make your quilting easier and more enjoyable, we encourage you to carefully read all of the general instructions, study the color photographs, and familiarize yourself with the individual project instructions before beginning a project.

FABRICS

SELECTING FABRICS

Choose high-quality, medium-weight 100% cotton fabrics. All-cotton fabrics hold a crease better, fray less, and are easier to quilt than cotton/polyester blends.

Yardage requirements listed for each project are based on 43"/44" wide fabric with a "usable" width of 40" after shrinkage and trimming selvages. Actual usable width will probably vary slightly from fabric to fabric. Our recommended yardage lengths should be adequate for occasional re-squaring of fabric when many cuts are required.

PREPARING FABRICS

Pre-washing fabrics may cause edges to ravel. As a result, your precut fabrics may not be large enough to cut all of the pieces required for your chosen projects. Therefore, we do not recommend pre-washing yardage or precut fabrics.

Before cutting, prepare fabrics with a steam iron set on cotton and starch or sizing. The starch or sizing will give the fabric a crisp finish. This will make cutting more accurate and may make piecing easier.

If no precut fabrics are being used you may choose to pre-wash, dry, and press your fabrics before cutting. If fabrics are not pre-washed, washing the finished wall hanging will cause shrinkage and give it a more "antiqued" look and feel. Bright and dark colors, which may run, should always be washed before cutting. After washing and drying fabric, fold lengthwise with wrong sides together and matching selvages.

ROTARY CUTTING

- Place fabric on work surface with fold closest to you.
- Cut all strips from the selvage-to-selvage width of the fabric unless otherwise indicated in project instructions.
- Square left edge of fabric using rotary cutter and rulers (**Figs. 1-2**).

Fig. 1

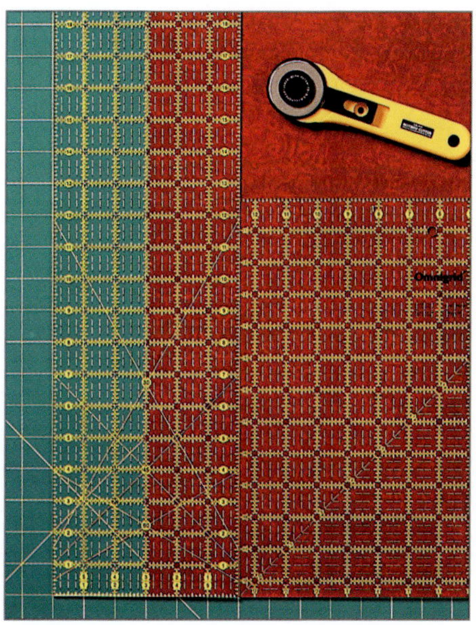

Fig. 2

- To cut each strip required for a project, place ruler over cut edge of fabric, aligning desired marking on ruler with cut edge; make cut (**Fig. 3**).

Fig. 3

- When cutting several strips from a single piece of fabric, it is important to make sure that cuts remain at a perfect right angle to the fold; square fabric as needed.

MAKING AND USING TEMPLATES

1. To make a template from a pattern, use a permanent fine-point pen and a ruler to carefully trace pattern onto template plastic. Cut out template along inner edge of drawn line. Check template against original pattern for accuracy.
2. Place template face down on wrong side of fabric. Use a fabric-marking pen to draw around template. Cut out fabric piece using scissors or rotary cutting equipment.

MACHINE PIECING

Precise cutting, followed by accurate piecing, will ensure that all pieces of wall hanging top fit together well.

- Set sewing machine stitch length for approximately 11 stitches per inch.
- Use neutral-colored general-purpose sewing thread (not quilting thread) in needle and in bobbin.

- An accurate $^{1}/_{4}$" seam allowance is *essential*. Presser feet that are $^{1}/_{4}$" wide are available for most sewing machines.

- When piecing, always place pieces right sides together and match raw edges; pin if necessary.

- Chain piecing saves time and will usually result in more accurate piecing.

- Trim away points of seam allowances that extend beyond edges of sewn pieces.

SEWING STRIP SETS

When there are several strips to assemble into a strip set, first sew strips together into pairs, then sew pairs together to form strip set. To help avoid distortion, sew seams in opposite directions **(Fig. 4)**.

SEWING ACROSS SEAM INTERSECTIONS

When sewing across intersection of two seams, place pieces right sides together and match seams exactly, making sure seam allowances are pressed in opposite directions **(Fig. 5)**.

SEWING SHARP POINTS

To ensure sharp points when joining triangular or diagonal pieces, stitch across the center of the "X" (shown in pink) formed on wrong side by previous seams **(Fig. 6)**.

Fig. 4

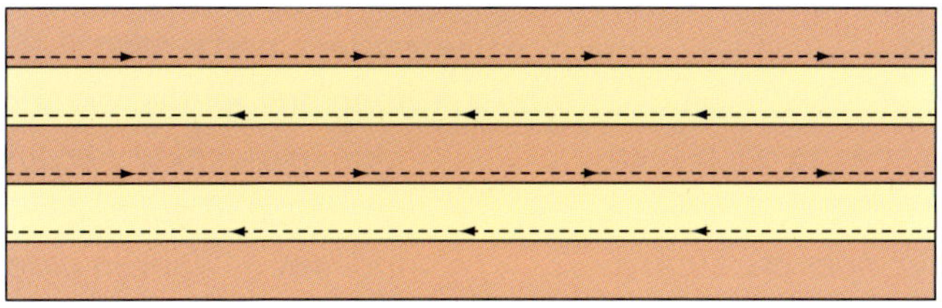

Fig. 5

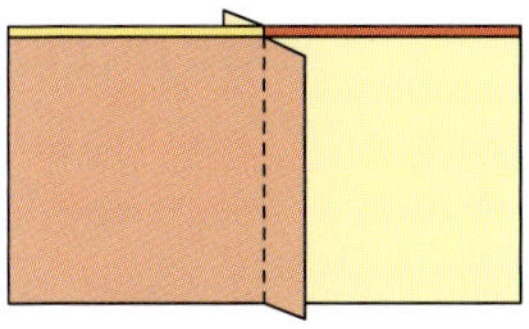

Fig. 6

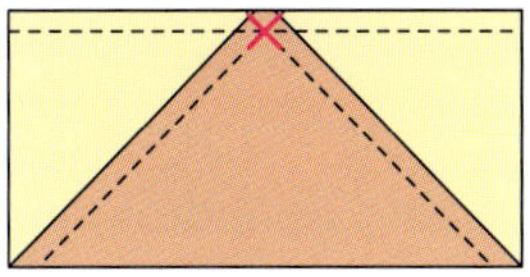

PRESSING

- Use steam iron set on "Cotton" for all pressing.
- Press after sewing each seam.
- Seam allowances are almost always pressed to one side, usually toward darker fabric. However, to reduce bulk it may occasionally be necessary to press seam allowances toward the lighter fabric or even to press them open.
- To prevent dark fabric seam allowance from showing through light fabric, trim darker seam allowance slightly narrower than lighter seam allowance.
- To press long seams, such as those in long strip sets, without curving or other distortion, lay strips across width of the ironing board.
- When sewing blocks into rows, seam allowances may be pressed in one direction in odd numbered rows and in the opposite direction in even numbered rows. When sewing rows together, press seam allowances in one direction.

QUILTING

Quilting holds the three layers (top, batting, and backing) of the wall hanging together and can be done by hand or machine. Because marking, layering, and quilting are interrelated and may be done in different orders depending on circumstances, please read entire ***Quilting*** *section, pages 58-59, before beginning project.*

MARKING QUILTING LINES

Quilting lines may be marked using fabric marking pencils, chalk markers, or water- or air-soluble pens.

Simple quilting designs may be marked with chalk or chalk pencil after basting. A small area may be marked, then quilted, before moving to next area to be marked. Intricate designs should be marked before basting using a more durable marker.

Caution: Pressing may permanently set some marks. **Test** different markers **on scrap fabric** to find one that marks clearly and can be thoroughly removed.

CHOOSING THE BATTING

The appropriate batting will make quilting easier. For fine hand quilting, choose low-loft batting. All cotton or cotton/polyester blend battings work well for machine quilting because the cotton helps "grip" quilt layers. If wall hanging is to be tied, a high-loft batting, sometimes called extra-loft or fat batting, may be used to make wall hanging "fluffy."

Types of batting include cotton, polyester, wool, cotton/polyester blend, cotton/wool blend, and silk.

When selecting batting, refer to package labels for characteristics and care instructions. Cut batting same size as prepared backing.

ASSEMBLING THE WALL HANGING

1. Examine wrong side of wall hanging top closely; trim any seam allowances and clip any threads that may show through front of the wall hanging. Press wall hanging top, being careful not to "set" any marked quilting lines.
2. Place backing *wrong* side up on flat surface. Use masking tape to tape edges of backing to surface. Place batting on top of backing fabric. Smooth batting gently, being careful not to stretch or tear. Center wall hanging top *right* side up on batting.
3. Use 1" rustproof safety pins to "pin-baste" all layers together, spacing pins approximately 4" apart. Begin at center and work toward outer edges to secure all layers. If possible, place pins away from areas that will be quilted, although pins may be removed as needed when quilting.

MACHINE QUILTING METHODS

Use general-purpose thread in bobbin. Do not use quilting thread. Thread the needle of machine with general-purpose thread or transparent monofilament thread to make quilting blend with wall hanging top fabrics. Use decorative thread, such as a metallic or contrasting-color general-purpose thread, to make quilting lines stand out more.

Straight-Line Quilting

The term "straight-line" is somewhat deceptive, since curves (especially gentle ones) as well as straight lines can be stitched with this technique.

1. Set stitch length for six to ten stitches per inch and attach walking foot to sewing machine.
2. Determine which section of wall hanging will have longest continuous quilting line, oftentimes area from center top to center bottom. Roll up and secure each edge of wall hanging to help reduce the bulk, keeping fabrics smooth. Smaller projects may not need to be rolled.
3. Begin stitching on longest quilting line, using very short stitches for the first 1/4" to "lock" quilting. Stitch across project, using one hand on each side of walking foot to slightly spread fabric and to guide fabric through machine. Lock stitches at end of quilting line.
4. Continue machine quilting, stitching longer quilting lines first to stabilize wall hanging before moving on to other areas.

Free-Motion Quilting

Free-motion quilting may be free form or may follow a marked pattern.

1. Attach darning foot to sewing machine and lower or cover feed dogs.
2. Position wall hanging under darning foot; lower foot. Holding top thread, take a stitch and pull bobbin thread to top of wall hanging. To "lock" beginning of quilting line, hold top and bobbin threads while making three to five stitches in place.
3. Use one hand on each side of darning foot to slightly spread fabric and to move fabric through the machine. Even stitch length is achieved by using smooth, flowing hand motion and steady machine speed. Slow machine speed and fast hand movement will create long stitches. Fast machine speed and slow hand movement will create short stitches. Move wall hanging sideways, back and forth, in a circular motion, or in a random motion to create desired designs; do not rotate wall hanging. Lock stitches at end of each quilting line.

MAKING A HANGING SLEEVE

Attaching a hanging sleeve to back of wall hanging before the binding is added allows project to be displayed on wall.

1. Measure width of wall hanging top edge and subtract 1". Cut piece of fabric 7"w by determined measurement.
2. Press short edges of fabric piece $^{1}/_{4}$" to wrong side; press edges $^{1}/_{4}$" to wrong side again and machine stitch in place.
3. Matching wrong sides, fold piece in half lengthwise to form a tube.
4. Follow project instructions to sew binding to wall hanging top and to trim backing and batting. Before Blindstitching binding to backing, match raw edges and stitch hanging sleeve to center top edge on back of wall hanging.
5. Finish binding wall hanging, treating hanging sleeve as part of backing.
6. Blindstitch bottom of hanging sleeve to backing, taking care not to stitch through to front of wall hanging.

BINDING

Binding encloses the raw edges of wall hanging. Because of its stretchiness, bias binding works well for binding projects with curves or rounded corners and tends to lie smooth and flat in any given circumstance. Binding may also be cut from straight lengthwise or crosswise grain of fabric.

MAKING CONTINUOUS BIAS STRIP BINDING

Bias strips for binding can simply be cut and pieced to desired length. However, when a long length of binding is needed, the "continuous" method is quick and accurate.

1. Cut square from binding fabric the size indicated in project instructions. Cut square in half diagonally to make two triangles.
2. With right sides together and using $^{1}/_{4}$" seam allowance, sew triangles together **(Fig. 7)**; press seam allowances open.

Fig. 7

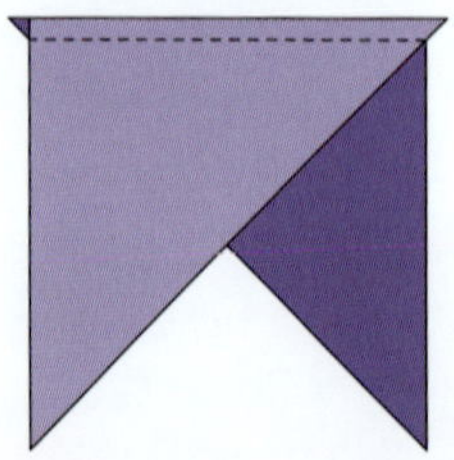

3. On wrong side of fabric, draw lines the width of binding as specified in project instructions, usually $2^{1}/_{2}$" **(Fig. 8)**. Cut off any remaining fabric less than this width.

Fig. 8

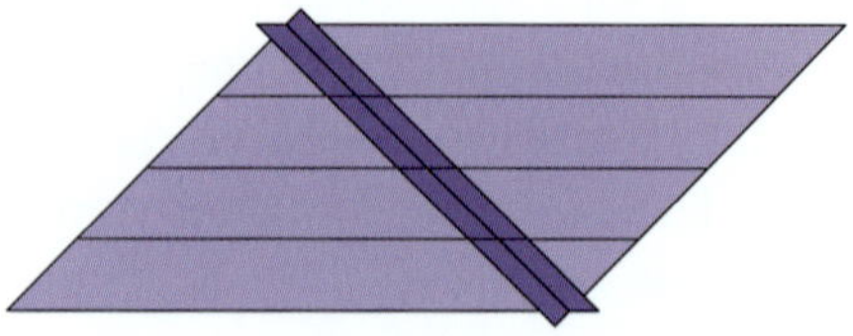

4. With right sides inside, bring short edges together to form tube; match raw edges so that first drawn line of top section meets second drawn line of bottom section **(Fig. 9)**.

Fig. 9

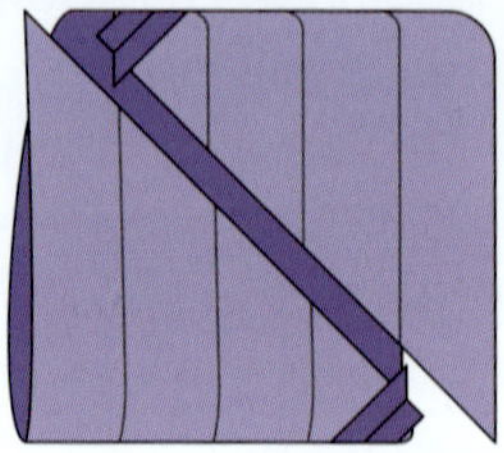

5. Carefully pin edges together by inserting pins through drawn lines at point where drawn lines intersect, making sure pins go through intersections on both sides. Using 1/4" seam allowance, sew edges together; press seam allowances open.
6. To cut continuous strip, begin cutting along first drawn line **(Fig. 10)**. Continue cutting along drawn line around tube.

Fig. 10

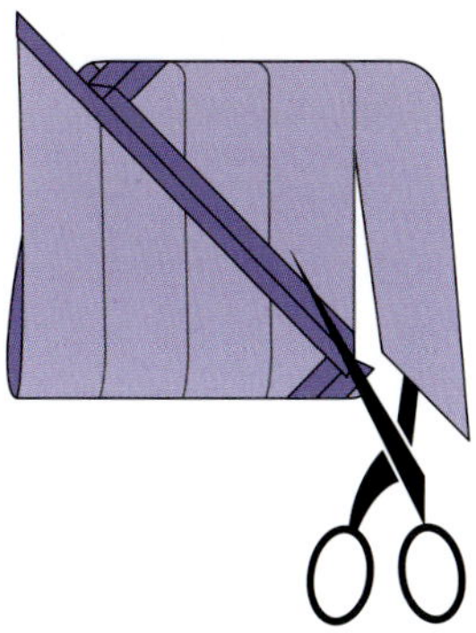

7. Trim ends of bias strip square.
8. Matching wrong sides and raw edges, carefully press bias strip in half lengthwise to complete binding.

MAKING STRAIGHT-GRAIN BINDING

1. Cut crosswise strips of binding fabric the determined length and the width called for in project instructions.
2. Sew strips together using a diagonal seam **(Fig. 11)**.

Fig. 11

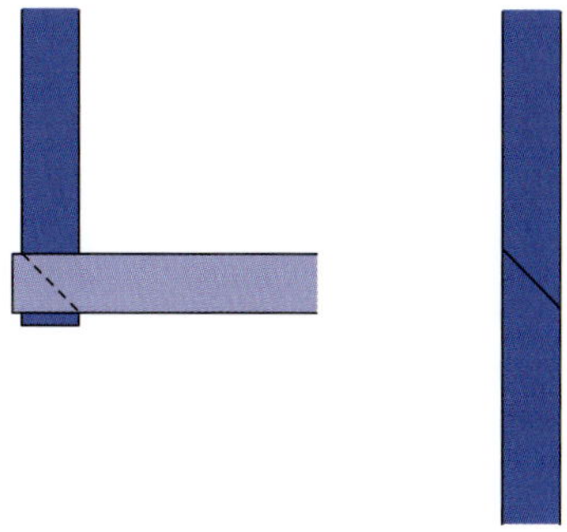

3. Matching wrong sides and raw edges, press strip(s) in half lengthwise to complete binding.

ATTACHING BINDING WITH MITERED CORNERS

1. Beginning with one end near center on bottom edge of wall hanging, lay binding around wall hanging to make sure that seams in binding will not end up at a corner. Adjust placement if necessary. Matching raw edges of binding to raw edge of wall hanging top, pin binding to right side of wall hanging along one edge.
2. When you reach first corner, mark 1/4" from corner of wall hanging top **(Fig. 12)**.

Fig. 12

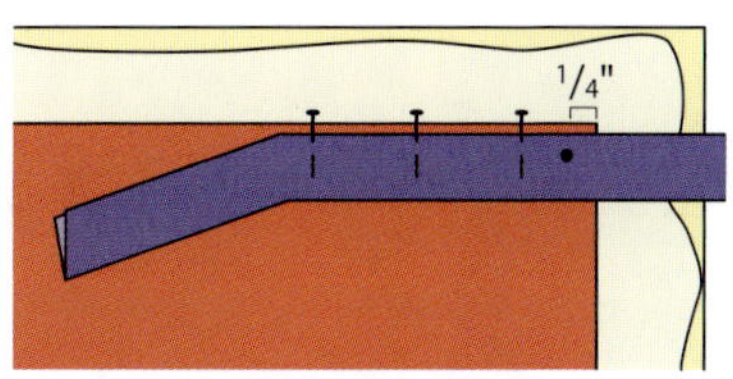

3. Beginning approximately 10" from end of binding and using 1/4" seam allowance, sew binding to wall hanging, backstitching at beginning of stitching and at mark **(Fig. 13)**. Lift needle out of fabric and clip thread.

Fig. 13

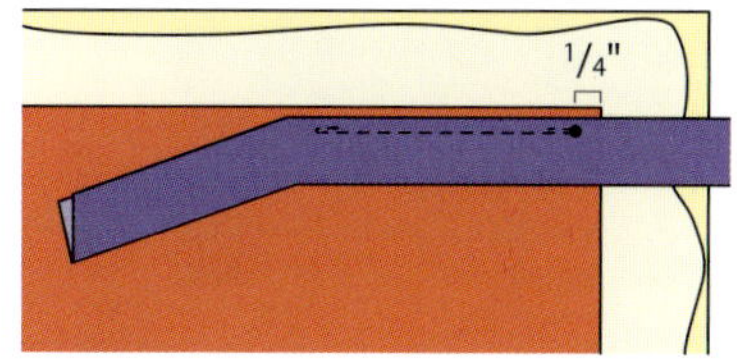

4. Fold binding as shown in **Figs. 14-15** and pin binding to adjacent side, matching raw edges. When you've reached the next corner, mark 1/4" from edge of wall hanging top.

Fig. 14

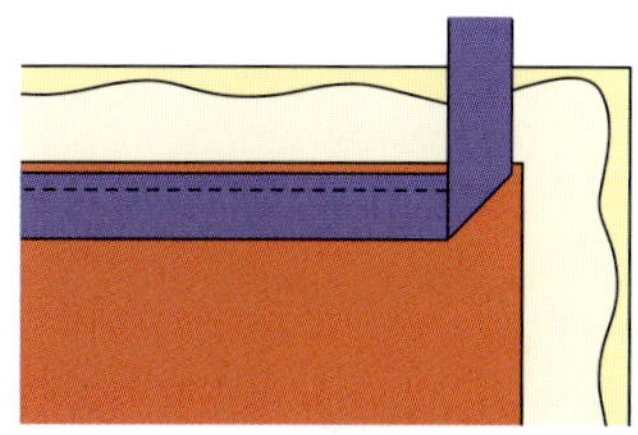

Fig. 15

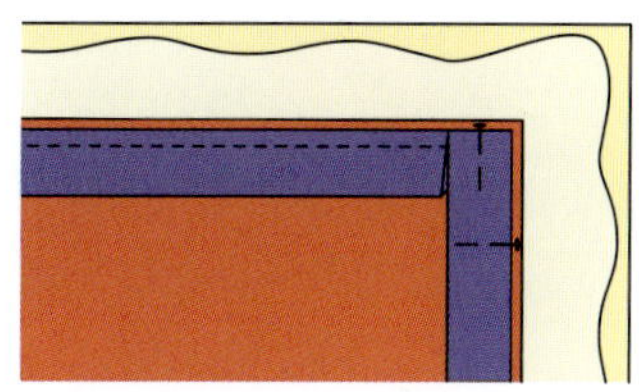

5. Backstitching at edge of wall hanging top, sew pinned binding to wall hanging **(Fig. 16)**; backstitch at the next mark. Lift needle out of fabric and clip thread.

Fig. 16

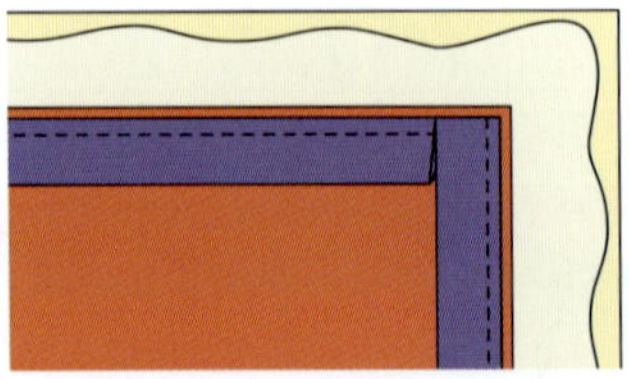

6. Continue sewing binding to wall hanging, stopping approximately 10" from starting point **(Fig. 17)**.

Fig. 17

7. Bring beginning and end of binding to center of opening and fold each end back, leaving a 1/4" space between folds **(Fig. 18)**. Finger press folds.

Fig. 18

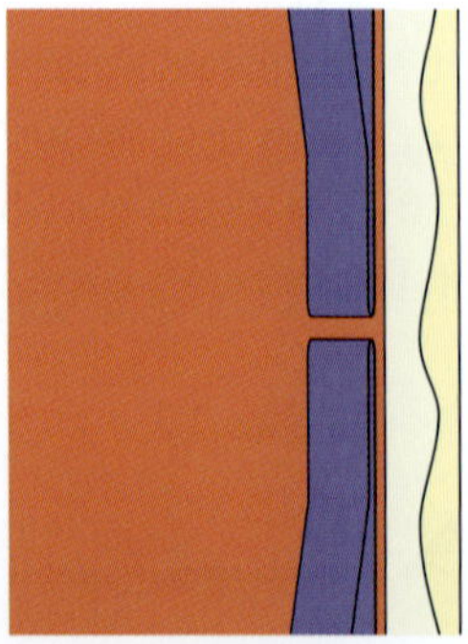

8. Unfold ends of binding and draw a line across wrong side in finger-pressed crease. Draw a line through the lengthwise pressed fold of binding at the same spot to create a cross mark. With edge of ruler at cross mark, line up 45˚ angle marking on ruler with one long side of binding. Draw a diagonal line from edge to edge. Repeat on remaining end, making sure that the two diagonal lines are angled the same way **(Fig. 19)**.

Fig. 19

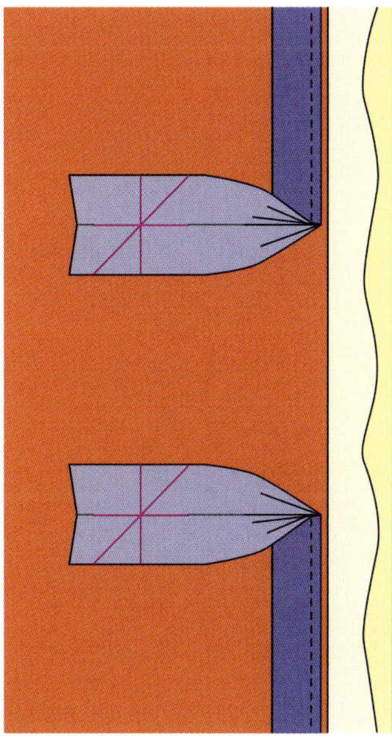

9. Matching right sides and diagonal lines, pin binding ends together at right angles **(Fig. 20)**.

Fig. 20

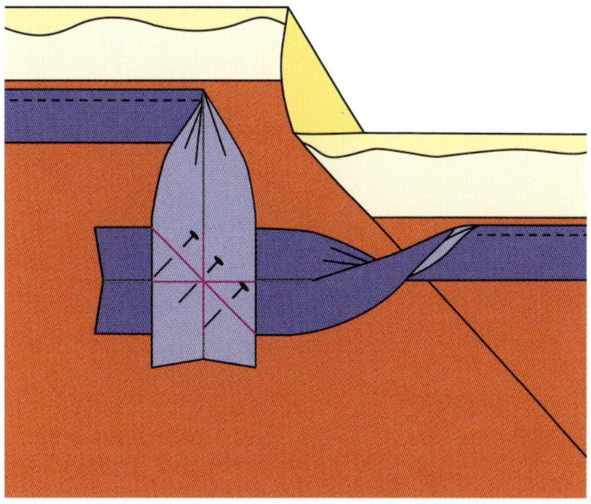

10. Machine stitch along diagonal line **(Fig. 21)**, removing pins as you stitch.

Fig. 21

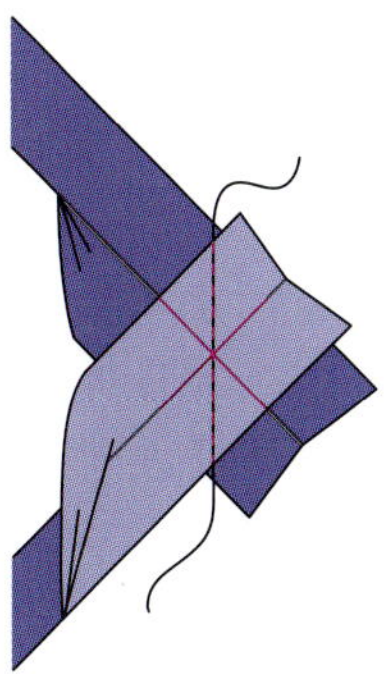

11. Lay binding against wall hanging to double check that it is correct length.
12. Trim binding ends, leaving 1/4" seam allowance; press seam open. Stitch binding to wall hanging.
13. Trim backing and batting a scant 1/4" larger than wall hanging top so that batting and backing will fill the binding when it is folded over to wall hanging backing. If using narrower binding, trim backing and batting even with edges of wall hanging top.
14. On one edge of wall hanging, fold binding over to wall hanging backing and pin pressed edge in place, covering stitching line **(Fig. 22)**. On adjacent side, fold binding over, forming a mitered corner **(Fig. 23)**. Repeat to pin remainder of binding in place.

Fig. 22

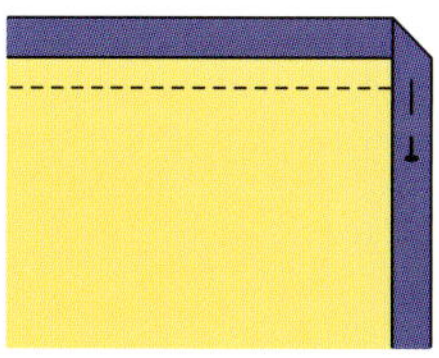

Fig. 23

15. Blindstitch binding to backing, taking care not to stitch through to front of wall hanging.

Metric Conversion Chart

Inches x 2.54 = centimeters (cm)	Yards x .9144 = meters (m)
Inches x 25.4 = millimeters (mm)	Yards x 91.44 = centimeters (cm)
Inches x .0254 = meters (m)	Centimeters x .3937 = inches (")
	Meters x 1.0936 = yards (yd)

Standard Equivalents

1/8"	3.2 mm	0.32 cm	1/8 yard	11.43 cm	0.11 m
1/4"	6.35 mm	0.635 cm	1/4 yard	22.86 cm	0.23 m
3/8"	9.5 mm	0.95 cm	3/8 yard	34.29 cm	0.34 m
1/2"	12.7 mm	1.27 cm	1/2 yard	45.72 cm	0.46 m
5/8"	15.9 mm	1.59 cm	5/8 yard	57.15 cm	0.57 m
3/4"	19.1 mm	1.91 cm	3/4 yard	68.58 cm	0.69 m
7/8"	22.2 mm	2.22 cm	7/8 yard	80 cm	0.8 m
1"	25.4 mm	2.54 cm	1 yard	91.44 cm	0.91 m

Production Team: Senior Graphic Artist - Lora Puls; Photographer - Jason Masters; and Photography Stylist – Lori Wenger.

We have made every effort to ensure that these instructions are accurate and complete. We cannot, however, be responsible for human error, typographical mistakes, or variations in individual work.

Made in U.S.A.

Library of Congress Control Number: 2019941818